ANOTHER SELF

ANOTHER SELF

James Lees-Milne

With an introduction by Jeremy Lewis

A COMMON READER EDITION
THE AKADINE PRESS

JH

Another Self

A COMMON READER EDITION published 2000 by The Akadine Press, Inc.,
by arrangement with John Murray (Publishers) Ltd.

A COMMON READER EDITION and fountain colophon are trademarks
of The Akadine Press, Inc.

ISBN 1-58579-008-7

10 9 8 7 6 5 4 3 2 1

To
ROSAMOND LEHMANN

CONTENTS

	Introduction by Jeremy Lewis	ix
I	TOBIAS AND THE ANGEL	I
II	SHE	25
III	HE	41
IV	THEY	61
V	THEO	82
VI	MAGDALEN TO MAFRA	98
VII	BANDITS AND BEASTS	124
VIII	MARS ULTOR	150

INTRODUCTION

I first met James Lees-Milne – or 'Jim', as I was eventually emboldened to call him – in the early 1980s, when I was working as an editor with Chatto & Windus. As well as publishing a novel and a biography of his old friend Harold Nicolson, Chatto had launched the first two volumes of his diaries, in which he described how, after being invalided out of the army in September 1941, he had rejoined the National Trust, and spent the war years trundling up and down the country in his baby Austin interviewing the owners of remote and dilapidated country houses, many of which were saved for the nation as a result of his endeavours. Some of the country house owners were eccentric to the point of lunacy, and Lees-Milne had a keen eye for their foibles; I thought his diaries far and away the most entertaining I had ever read, relishing their combination of self-deprecation, comicality and – back in London between forays – feline literary and social gossip, much of it to do with Ivy Compton-Burnett and her companion, Margaret Jourdain, and a satanic publisher called Charles Fry. Mr Lees-Milne was a close friend of the then boss of Chatto, the terrifying Norah Smallwood, and since she was proprietorial about her authors it seemed unlikely that I would ever meet my hero in the flesh; nor was I sure that I wanted to, since writers are often best encountered only in print.

Jim decided to leave Chatto after Norah retired, but in the aftermath of her departure I found myself acting, briefly, as his editor, working with him on *The Last Stuarts*, a study of the Old and Young Pretenders' melancholy lives in exile, and *Caves of Ice*, Volume Three of the diaries, which takes his perambulations on into the post-war years. He was, as I remember, a model author – quick, efficient, open to advice (not that much was called for) and unlikely to take offence at one's suggestions, unless too obviously half-baked. What I particularly enjoyed about him – and here he differed greatly from the more pompous, self-important kind of writer – was the great gulf set between the way in which he presented himself, and what he actually achieved. He had spent his life as a hard-working, highly professional author whose scholarship, however lightly worn, was entirely genuine and would put many a leaden academic to shame; yet he liked to present himself as a bumbling, ineffectual fellow, bordering on senility at times, whose reputation as an authority on architecture and country houses, and talents as a biographer, were almost certainly undeserved. 'Oh dear no, I'm far too gaga,' I can hear him saying when I urged him to bring out another volume of diaries: but that was at least three volumes ago, and in the meantime he has treated us as well to – among other items – lives of Lord Esher and the 6th Duke of Devonshire, and the masterly *Fourteen Friends*, in which he looks back, with affection, humour and the occasional dash of asperity, on such friends as Osbert Lancaster, Henry Green, Robert Byron, Rosamond Lehmann and James Pope-Hennessy. Jim is sometimes accused of being a snob, but among his many virtues as a writer – and one that he shares with his fellow-Etonian Cyril Connolly – is an ability to articulate feelings and failings common to us all, so that one's reading is interrupted by familiar starts of recognition.

Encountered in the gloomy, labyrinthine corridors of the old Chatto building, so reminiscent of a prep school or an old-fashioned lunatic asylum, or over lunch at Brooks's, or in his honey-coloured house by the gates of Badminton House, Jim proved nothing like as alarming as Norah would have had us believe. A tall, elegant, rather dandified figure, clad in unusual jackets and wearing a silk foulard at the neck, he has a long, humorous face and a soft, hesitant voice: a slight suggestion of a stammer adds to the import – and comicality – of what he has to say. Like many of the best writers, he has a gift for the embellished or suitably heightened anecdote, delivered in an appropriately dead-pan voice; despite the occasional outbursts of fury or revenge recorded in *Another Self*, his manners are impeccable. I have met him far less often than I would have wished, but there is no one whose good opinion I value more.

Originally published by Hamish Hamilton in 1970, *Another Self* is brief and episodic, taking us from his childhood in Worcestershire through Eton and Oxford and employment with Lord Lloyd to his leaving the army, at which point the diaries take up the story. It is almost certainly the funniest autobiography ever written, but readers with too literal a cast of mind should probably give it a miss. Indeed, I have often used *Another Self*, along with Patrick Leigh Fermor's two books about his pre-war walk from Rotterdam to Istanbul, as a litmus test, designed to smoke out kindred spirits with tastes similar to my own; and just as, very occasionally, one comes across some unromantic soul who objects to Leigh Fermor on the prosaic ground that he couldn't possibly remember in quite such persuasive detail the events of sixty years ago, so some dim spirits grumble about the implausibility of *Another Self*, with particular reference to Lees-Milne's account of how he short-sightedly marched a platoon of Guards over the cliffs of Dover, leaving them clinging to outcrops of chalk and tufts of grass, or how the bottom fell out of the clapped-out horse-drawn carriage in which he and his mother arrived at his prep school, so forcing them to run round and round the circular drive until the cabby could bring his vehicle to a halt.

The finest comic set-piece of all describes Lees-Milne's unhappy dealings with that wasp-like martinet Sir Roderick Jones, husband to Enid Bagnold and the then Chairman of Reuters: office-workers who have suffered under the tyrant's lash will scarce forebear to cheer as Sir Roderick's secretary takes his revenge on the pompous little monster, whose only hope of immortality lies –

by a further twist of the knife – in these pages. Like all the best comedy, though, *Another Self* is tinged with sadness: some of its most poignant moments deal – with a kind of rueful regret – with lost or unrequited love; and the jokes and the self-deprecation are combined with a hatred of the modern world, and a terrible anger at the way in which so many beautiful things, from country houses to the Roman Mass, have been abandoned or destroyed. In an appalling scene, Lees-Milne describes how, as a generally unhappy undergraduate at Magdalen, he visited Rousham, a beautiful eighteenth-century house on the Cherwell, and stood impotently by while its then tenant, a rich, half-mad philistine, flicked at the paintings with a riding-crop and took pot-shots at the statues in the garden: from that moment, he tells us, he decided to dedicate his life to preserving the 'infinitely fragile and precious' buildings of England, for they 'meant to me then, and have meant ever since, far more than human lives'. Such sentiments could hardly be less politically correct. They are matched only by his regret that – given his hatred of Communism, and his love for the Catholic Church as it was – he never fought for Franco during the Spanish Civil War. Equally unfashionable is his delight in class distinctions, which he rightly regards as 'a chief ingredient of the world's greatest fiction'. Class barriers, on the other hand, he finds abhorrent, and welcomes their diminution.

Autobiography is an art at which the English have excelled in the post-war years, and the best of them – Julian Maclaren-Ross's *Memoirs of the Forties*, John Gale's *Clean Young Englishman*, T. C. Worsley's *Flannelled Fool*, and the memoirs of Michael Wharton and Alan Ross – combine comicality with a sense of the sad absurdity of life, a delight in the oddities of human behaviour with a deceptive authorial modesty. *Another Self* is perhaps the finest of them all, a small masterpiece that remains as fresh and funny and wise as ever.

JEREMY LEWIS
1998

I

TOBIAS AND THE ANGEL

M Y WORLD was the only real world. Nothing about it seemed incongruous; and those events which happened in it were never inconsequential. Its relation with the great outside world was tenuous. By which I do not deny that a few of my notable fancies were sparked off by momentous contacts with the unreal, outside world. For of course they often were. A riveting story or a glamorous present might do the trick, and set the magic working. On the other hand the pattern of events in my world was often outrageously disturbed by trivial demands made by the unreal world, such as to eat tapioca pudding, to wash my teeth, or to go to bed when I felt disinclined. With time I learnt how to condition these extraneous demands, and prevent them from totally dislocating the even flow of the true inner existence. In other words I learnt to master them.

On the whole how very satisfactory the real existence was. Instead of being the victim of circumstance, which I have ever since been, I was its creator. I could make it take any turn I liked. I am at a loss to explain how I managed this, because the power to do so left me quite half a century ago. The closest parallel to the experience is the siesta dream. On a hot drowsy afternoon on the Mediterranean after a heavy luncheon with red wine I can still lie down and actually conjure up my own dreams. By an imperceptible process of thought I can spin them into whatever shape I want. I daresay that certain drugs are even more conducive to these results than *filet de boeuf* and two glasses of Médoc consumed at midday in the height of summer. But I have reason for knowing that many will invoke even nastier dreams than those that come in an ordinary night's sleep, dreams over which we have no control at all.

My siesta dreams, like so many experiences of my inner life before the age of ten, when this particular life began to disintegrate, are, I now recognize, part of the eternal search which I still conduct with ever decreasing success. I mean that the goal for ever recedes and is becoming so blurred as to be hardly recognizable. But when I was a very small child it was quite distinct, and only barely out of reach. My persistent 'day dreaming', as my poor parents called it, was a serious worry to them. Just as some children cannot coordinate their thoughts in words, and some their words on paper, but are otherwise normal, I could not for a longer time than usual concentrate on what I was supposed to be doing. I repeat the word 'supposed', because I could perfectly well concentrate upon and carry out whatever I set myself to perform. My mother, hoping that I would 'grow out of it', made excuses for me. My father was quite certain I was mad, and used to explain why to anyone who was interested enough to listen.

I was a deeply religious child. I am a religious sexagenarian without, I am afraid, being consistently devout. Why I am so I have no idea, because my father's attitude to religion was perfunctory. My mother's was at first indifferent, and in her middle and old age positively hostile. God, she would declare before the last war, was no better than a nuisance; and during the war indistinguishable from Hitler. In nursery days therefore religion was never thrust upon me. On the contrary it was, if not exactly withheld, certainly not fostered. And had I for instance expressed an ambition to take holy orders, both parents would have been profoundly shocked and discouraging.

Notwithstanding my parents' sentiments on religion, church played an extremely important part in their early married life and in my childhood. In the first place our church happened to be plumb in the middle of the manor garden. Secondly, attendance at divine service was a universally recognized means of giving vent to that community spirit, which before the First World War was very compulsive in remote country districts. Everyone who was anyone in the village automatically assembled once a week, and offered up his and her praise and thanksgiving as much to the prevailing social system as to the Almighty. Our family was no exception in rejoicing that the happy state of the world was what it was. So my parents did not regard spending one hour a week glorifying the *status quo* as too great a sacrifice of their leisure moments.

I cannot remember a stage of my life at home when I did not go to church. Before I could walk I was carried there by my nurse, dumped on the floor of the pew, and allowed to make castles out of hassocks and prayer books. The ritual was always the same. Mrs. Hartwell began pealing the bell a quarter of an hour before service. She was sexton, verger and cleaner combined. She was an aged widow who gallantly brought up an orphaned brood of undisciplined grandchildren. She was tiny, about four foot nothing, with skin and sinews creased and stretched like the parchment leaves of a family bible. Her face was remarkable for an expansive smile sewn from one ear to the other, and watery blue eyes which she constantly wiped with a duster. She was never to be seen – but once – without a huge hat which practically concealed her like an umbrella. The brim was covered with leaves and cherries of purple celluloid, which her grandchildren would pop during those brief intervals when she dozed off in her pew. But for most of the service she was scuttling to and fro like a minute, friendly rat, in one hand her duster, in the other a broom whose bristles were worn away to memories. She smelled of linseed.

Although really far too old and frail, Mrs. Hartwell refused to relinquish the bell rope with its fluffy stripes in red, white and blue, called I believe the "sally". She regarded the pulling of it as her sacred duty, which she would surrender to no one, until the breath, as she put it, was out of her body. The act was sometimes attended by alarming manifestations. For bell ringing, even with one rope, necessitates a sense of rhythm in the ringer. Mrs. Hartwell lacked

3

this sense. Occasionally she would pull too soon, or too late. The rope thereupon gave a jerk and if she failed to let go – it was not in her nature to let go of things – she would be swept up the belfry. When this happened she would either cling to the rope until it came down again, or she would swing on it until her feet touched a ladder kept permanently fixed to the wall to enable workmen or builders to go up the tower. With astonishing agility for a person of her years she would scramble down the ladder and resume ringing as though nothing had happened.

Once, having been carried upwards, she failed for some reason to swing across to the ladder. Owing to the unusual velocity of her ascent the whole mechanism of the bell became dislocated, and the rope did not come down again. Mrs. Hartwell was left clinging to a small fraction of the fluffy part which was stuck in the hole of the ceiling some thirty feet above the ground. She looked like one of those mediaeval saints in a state of levitation. Beneath a voluminous skirt and petticoats her button boots could be observed going through the motions of someone trying desperately and ineffectually to swim. The impact of her poor head against the ceiling had dislodged the purple umbrella of cherries, which floated pathetically to the floor. Yet no cry of alarm escaped her. The congregation anxiously gathered under the tower and began shouting contradictory directions how she was on no account to let go. With much presence of mind the Vicar ran to fetch Haines, our chauffeur, to come to the rescue. My mother, whose behaviour in a crisis was unpredictable, called loudly for a grappling iron. 'Whatever's that, m'm?' somebody asked. 'I don't know,' was her answer. Determined, nevertheless, to offer encouragement, if nothing else, she kept repeating, 'It's all right, Mrs. Hartwell. You've nothing to worry about. I've got your hat,' which was scant consolation to a septuagenarian clinging to an inch of rope for dear life. Eventually Haines, when found, was able by climbing through the trap-door in the ceiling to release the rope, which had got jammed in the wheel of the bell. Slowly Mrs. Hartwell was lowered into the font. Quite undeterred by this mishap she shook herself, put on her hat and began pulling the rope all over again.

The congregation, even before 1914, was not unduly large. For years the same people attended church. Invariably they sat in the same places. In fact I believe newcomers, whenever there were any, must have been allocated pews – or benches as the case might be – by someone, presumably the Vicar, according to their station in the village hierarchy. Most of the places were of course inherited, but by what precise right no one had ever questioned. It was one of those unwritten, but nonetheless divine rights which meant so much to British people up to very recent times.

On the south side of the nave was a row of high box pews. The foremost, up against the chancel arch, was the manor pew. It was distinguished from the others – the crest on the door panel was now practically obliterated – by red plush squabs on the hard upright seats. In the corner by the door was a pile of calf and suède-bound prayer books, quarto size, with the names of their 18th and early 19th century owners stamped on the covers. They were a joy to handle. When opened they gave out a sweet smell of the dust and must of past ages. Their thick, yellowing leaves were printed with f's instead of s's. Others were of tortoiseshell with silver spines and hinges. On top of the pile was regularly placed by Mrs. Hartwell the embroidered collection bag for my father to hand round. Behind our pew came four others of slightly lesser dimensions, and with no squabs on the bare benches, as befitted their occupants, who were farmers and small householders.

On the north side of the nave immediately opposite the manor pew was the three-decker, consisting of reading desk, clerk's stall and pulpit. Each had a door which it was Mrs. Hartwell's privilege and pride to open and shut noisily throughout the service. Beneath the three-decker was the Vicarage pew, which was not boxed or particularly comfortable. Within the chancel, practically hidden from view, were two benches along the south wall facing the monuments and the harmonium. They were reserved for the choir, which consisted of Emily Empey, my mother's old governess, wrapped in a fawn teddy-bear coat and distant sanctity, and a knowing rather than knowledgeable schoolmistress from the neighbouring village. These two ladies led the singing in shrill falsetto. The last kept her beady eyes firmly fixed on the back of Mr Swift astride a stool at the harmonium. This extremely ugly instrument, which had been manufactured in Huddersfield in the 1870s, was encased in yellow pitch pine, and plastered with Gothic frets, spikes and dummy pipes. The damp had so affected the mechanism that only a few of the real pipes played at all. Mr Swift was not an accomplished executant. He was unable to bring out the best that was still left in the harmonium. Nor was his attention always on the ball, so to speak. He constantly forgot to play the Amen to the Vicar's prayers. When towards the end of a prayer the schoolmistress, whose ears were sharp, did not detect a preliminary wheeze from the pedals, she sensed that Mr Swift had lapsed into a reverie. While the Vicar waited, for he was a great stickler for rights, she would either throw a prayer book at Mr Swift's shoulder blades or, when the ammunition was exhausted, by putting two fingers in her mouth give out a piercing whistle as though hailing a taxi cab. Mr Swift's other weakness was to miscalculate the number of verses in the hymns. He would either stop short far too soon or continue playing long after the congregation had closed their hymnbooks and sat down.

As I have said, procedure at church was always the same. My parents would come in long after everyone else was seated. My mother would tiptoe down the nave as though to make amends for being late, smiling to left and right of her. My father would stalk behind, frowning. My sister, brother and I followed them in demure silence.

However late the family were, the Vicar could be relied upon to be later. After a long pause he would breathlessly gallop up the nave, his starched surplice dusting the tops of the pews in his wake. Genially he would halt to ask us which hymns we would like. If, and only if, my father were not present, he might ask what lessons we fancied. But the choice of lessons was my father's absolutely, whenever he did attend church. Sometimes the Vicar would chat, seemingly for hours. I can hear now the sizzle of his rubber soles as on winter mornings he loitered on the flagstones, between the regular cracks of which gusts of furry air billowed from the heating system patented in the 1840s, while the rest of us waited huddled in greatcoats and blowing on frozen fingers. My father would be enraged by these delaying tactics, which he imagined were directed against himself, and I am quite sure his extraordinary choice of Old Testament lessons was a means of getting his own back on the Vicar.

The service was in truth a pitched battle between the two. First one and then the other would be worsted. Occasionally my mother joined in to separate them. For the Vicar and my father had very different temperaments. Each exasperated the other. Each feared and yet respected the other. My father feared the Vicar's sanctity. The Vicar feared my father's aggressive practicality. He was a dear, sweet, woolly-minded scholar. He lived in a large, rambling rectory with his domineering mother-in-law, gentle wife and two ailing children, whom he supported on a miserable stipend. He longed for the congenial society of the senior common room, and his single annual outing was to the gaudy at his old Oxford College. Yet this unworldly, learned and lonely clergyman was tolerant, except of one thing, betting. He profoundly disapproved of racing and his cup of misery overflowed when my father presented the church with a new roof, new panelling or lighting, out of his winnings. This put the Vicar in a terrible predicament because he dared not refuse the gift, the acceptance of which went so much against the grain. I don't suppose my father would for a moment have paid the slightest attention if the Vicar had refused it. For he regarded the church, because it was in the garden, as his property, to do what he liked with. He never by any chance applied for a faculty before making alterations or putting up memorials; and was once extremely indignant when the Diocesan Committee dared to comment, after the event, upon his erection, without their permission, of a gallery across the west end. In the same way the Vicar, who was as poor as the proverbial church mouse, suffered agonies in not being able to decline the large tip which he knew my father added to the collection bag on Easter Day, and which he suspected to derive from the bookies. In fact my father carefully assessed his Easter offering according to the degree of his beastliness to the Vicar during the past twelve months. The nastier he imagined he had been, the more he gave by way of amends.

If the bush telegraph announced to the vicarage that my father had during the previous week won a race – if he lost the Vicar would be all smiles – Morning Prayer opened with the following sentence from Scripture: 'When the wicked man turneth away from his wickedness that he hath committed, and doeth that which is lawful and right, he shall save his soul alive.' The Vicar would read these words from his desk while looking my father sternly in the eye. The victim would visibly squirm in the manor pew. Not satisfied with this awful warning the Vicar would after a pause give the answer in a voice so like my father's as to be an unmistakable imitation, 'I acknowledge my transgressions, and my sin is ever before me.' All my father could do was to shake his head. In this way the Vicar won the first round.

Owing to Mr Swift's shortcomings the psalms were seldom chanted. The Vicar read the first verse and the congregation responded with the second, and so alternately. Or rather this is what should have happened. But the Vicar was so impatient that he never waited for the congregation to finish their verse before he started his next. Whereas everyone else gave up in a docile way, my father stoutly resisted. He would finish his response on rising notes of exasperation. Thus while the Vicar was gabbling, 'Lord, how long shall the ungodly triumph?' my father was still deliberately enunciating, 'Arise thou Judge of the world: and reward the proud after their deserving.' The Vicar had another annoying habit which my father considered downright insubordination. He would some- times take psalms that did not accord with the day of the month. My father would thereupon read out loud alternate verses of those that were on the calendar, and be quite unconcerned by the confusion that thereby ensued. The Vicar was also a trifle slapdash. Forty years in the same country parish were taking their toll of the spiritual rapture that had once distinguished him. In reading the prayer for the Royal Family from the ancient text before him, he would repeatedly invoke the fountain of all goodness to bless our gracious consort, Queen Charlotte, provoking my father to interpolate 'Mary', and after the words 'Princess of Wales' to add, 'There isn't one.'

But my father's great opportunity came with the lesson. This was when he actually took the stage, and could give as good as he got. In the first place an old bone of contention was that the Vicar would not allow him to read from the desk. Over this matter the Vicar displayed an uncharacteristic lack of charity, not to say dog-in-the-manger attitude. He was extremely jealous of the three-decker and would even hound Mrs Hartwell out of the clerk's stall to which, strictly speaking, she was entitled. He liked to use all three decks himself, although even he could not do so at the same time, and would bob about from one to the other, expecting Mrs Hartwell to open and shut the three doors before and after him. Therefore my father was obliged to stand rather ignominiously under the chancel arch, to which he would advance with impeccable dignity. He pointedly refused to make use of a modern lectern which the Vicar had offered as a compromise. He thought the offer insulting and the lectern a shoddy affair, which indeed it was. So he would hold the large bible in both hands, ostentatiously conveying to all of us how extremely awkward and heavy it was. On one occasion in a particularly vindictive mood he announced: 'Here beginneth the 36th chapter of the Book of Genesis, verses 1 to 43.'

After transfixing the Vicar in his turn with a steely eye, he started off: 'Now these are the generations of Esau, who is Edom. Esau took his wives of the daughters of Canaan; Adah the daughter of Elon the Hittite, and Aholibamah the daughter of Annah the daughter of Zibeon the Hivite; and Bashemath Ismael's daughter, sister of Nebajoth. And Adah bare to Esau, Eliphaz: and Bashemath bare Reuel.' On and on he droned. This was what he called enjoying his pound of flesh. First the farmers' wives, then Miss Empey, although so devout, then the schoolmistress dropped off, and last of all the servants from the manor at the risk of a severe reprimand after the service. Not so the Vicar. He shifted, took off his pince-nez, cleared his throat, and puffed out his cheeks to no avail. My father relentlessly continued: 'And the sons of Eliphaz were Teman, Omah, Zepho, and Gatam, and Kenaz. And Timna was concubine to Eliphaz, Esau's son. And these are the sons of Reuel; Nahath, and Zerah, Shammah and and Mizzah . . .' The Vicar becoming desperate made a sign for help to my mother who up to now had been remarkably patient. She nodded assent, and in her turn made signs to my father to stop. He took no notice and went on: 'And the children of Ezer are these; Bilhan, and Zaavan, and Achan; and of Dishan, Uz and Fuz. These are the dukes that came of the Horites; Duke Lotan, Duke Shobal, Duke Zibeon, Duke Anah.'

My mother could bear it no longer. She half rose in her seat, and making a face of pained embarrassment, mouthed the words, 'Your buttons!' while nodding a downward glance at my father's trousers. Instantly he turned scarlet, slid a hand across his stomach, and abruptly halted at the words, 'And the name of the city was Pau.' Mumbling, 'Here endeth the first lesson,' he sidled back into the pew. My mother was triumphant. She nudged him in the ribs and said, 'April fool!' My father looked perplexed. 'But it isn't April,' he retorted. 'It's August.'

*

In a perfectly uncomplicated way I believed in God, whole-heartedly. It has taken me years to learn that the reason for this implicit faith was that I never associated morals with him. In those days God was totally unrelated to justice, egalitarianism, righteous warfare, sexual abstinence, and those many other equivocal attributes with which holy people and theologians have invested him, so as to disguise a straightforward amalgam of goodness and beauty under a hopeless tangle of cross-purposes, and to obscure his clear countenance. When morals started to rear their beastly hydra heads the devil prompted me to question, speculate and finally lose my faith for a time. I found it impossible to reconcile conflicting codes of conduct with the ideal pacific being from whom I was told they emanated. At last I have succeeded in totally eliminating these thistles and nettles from my conscience. Once again God spreads his untrammelled, umbrageous branches like an oak tree over an eager tillage. No misinterpretations can confuse his purpose and growth in my heart.

In childhood then I accepted without question success or failure, joy or sorrow in that full measure with which they assail the pre-teenager. Although I accordingly rejoiced or suffered I never doubted the propriety of my being their object. I accepted God's treatment of me, nice or nasty, as part of the divine order of things. It never occurred to me to look for any motive behind their dispensation, or to consider myself undeservedly well or shabbily treated. No more than it occurred to me to be shocked by Jehovah's extraordinary notions of right and wrong, such as condonation of Lot's daughters lying with their aged father, and Samson's smiting one thousand silly, but harmless Philistines with the jawbone of an ass, or indeed his slaughter of poor Onan for a very venial weakness. I then looked, not dispassionately, but approvingly upon God as the dispenser of good and ill fortune alike in the way in which the ancient Greeks and Romans acknowledged the Olympian divinities as the wilful arbiters of their fate. My attitude was doubtless subservient and primitive, but not reprehensible. It was conditioned by that kind of love which a horse has for its rider, a slave for his master, and a child for his father. In the same spirit I accepted uncomplainingly until I was about ten – but not afterwards – my father's commands. As it happened the severe ones were usually mitigated by my mother's indulgence, a lovely factor which made it easy for me later in life to welcome mariology among the Catholic dogmas.

Until I was ten years old or thereabouts my life was a consistent, undeviating search for God, pure, simple and undefined. I was fortunately too young to read for myself the Old Testament, which unexpurgated is far more disturbing to adolescents than *Fanny Hill*. Instead I had to rely upon a selection of stories in a little book with a cover by Caldecott called, if I recollect rightly, *The Peep of Day*.

This book made the deepest impression upon me. I made my reluctant mother, who far preferred Hans Andersen, read it over and over again. No wonder she considered me a bit of a prig as I brushed aside every endeavour to listen for a change to *The Brave Tin Soldier*, or *The Beetle who went on his Travels*. No, it had to be the story of the infant Samuel, the angel who miraculously shielded those egregious bores Shadrach, Meshach and Abednego in the fiery furnace, Daniel in the lions' den, or Joseph through every phase of his goody-goody career. Freud may advance some complex reason why I identified myself with the hero in every case. I will offer my perfectly simple explanation. I craved the unattainable – notoriety. I longed to be admired by my father. Instead I was quite rightly ignored by him because I never showed a vestige of bravery on any possible occasion. And bravery was the chief virtue which could make a boy conspicuous in the sort of nursery from which the likes of myself sprang. This ineffectual, unfulfilled craving for recognition, first for bravery, then for any sort of achievement, persisted until I grew up. I would dream of stopping a runaway railway engine by throwing myself across the track, of flashing past the winning post on Derby Day, of taking curtain after curtain call at the Stratford-on-Avon pantomime, or of advising the King over an intimate cup of tea at Buckingham Palace how to deal with obstreperous suffragettes. Suddenly these infantine cravings left me, for I no longer cared. I had lost all interest in heroic achievement. Other false values, equally fatuous, took their place and in their turn were discarded.

While the *Peep of Day* influence lasted I made myself very tiresome by adopting the rôle of the various Old Testament heroes whose exploits my mother read to me. As the infant Samuel I would 'minister unto the Lord', which consisted in delivering myself of pious little dissertations in the servants' hall, and once accosting the Vicar as Eli the High Priest, and foretelling the total destruction of his house on account of the iniquity of his children (who incidentally were my own age and of spotless innocence). God had disclosed to me, I solemnly averred, that the manner of their destruction 'will make the ears of everyone that heareth it, tingle'. Such too was my ability to assume the rôle of a supernatural being that once as the fourth man, 'in form like the Son of God', I had to be forcibly prevented from walking into the nursery fire by the nursemaid and two of the household who, to my chagrin, declined to impersonate Shadrach, Meshach and Abednego. On another occasion during my Daniel-in-the-Lions'-Den rôle, I was found by the groom nestling in a loose-box between the legs of a particularly savage hunter. These were not acts of courage, but presumption, because I was absolutely convinced the Lord would not allow me to come to harm. Again my Joseph impersonation led to some awkward misunderstandings. I followed the example of Pharaoh's steward who put money and a silver cup into his brethren's sacks of corn, by surreptitiously opening the packed luggage of departing guests while they were at breakfast downstairs on Monday mornings, and throwing handfuls of coins – my mother always left money lying about – on top of their folded nightdresses. I even managed to jam into a full Gladstone bag the prized Hunt Cup won by my father at Cheltenham Races. Not until the owner of the luggage reached home and unpacked was this precious, but dented object revealed. His embarrassment must have been acute, and how he managed to explain it away in his bread-and-butter letter I never learned.

But far and away my favourite story was that of Tobias and the Angel. Because it came from the Apocrypha my mother affirmed that it could not, like the others, be strictly true. It was completely true to me. For months it held me enthralled. I never tired of hearing it read over and over again. I could think of little else. I lived with Tobias. I became Tobias. Precisely when I first identified myself with Tobias I do not recall. My childhood glimmers across the years through a tremulous haze of content, rather than unalloyed happiness, which gives it in retrospect a boundless, timeless quality like space. Fear, pain, grief and the other disagreeable emotions were transient visitations. Like summer thunder they made a noisy clamour, and quickly rolled away. Positive unhappiness was to come later in boyhood with school, spilling even into the holidays and staining all life with its sombre dye. The outstanding miseries which punctuated school life intoned like a funeral bell in the night the exact measurements of its hideous duration. But they were still in waiting.

The height of the Tobias fever must have coincided with the outbreak of war, for I clearly recall how news of that calamity broke upon our corner of Worcestershire. I was just six years old. I can see my father poring over the open sheets of the *Morning Post* at breakfast on presumably the 5th of August, 1914. It must have been a fine day because at this early hour his shirt sleeves were rolled up, which meant that he had already been gardening. I was squatting on the carpet, my eyes fascinated by the head and tongue on his forearm of the serpent which as a young man in Japan he had had tattooed all over his body. 'Good God!' he suddenly shouted. 'We have declared war on Germany.' He dropped the paper which fell across a plateful of toast and marmalade.

'Does that mean that we shan't get enough to eat?' I asked anxiously. No attention was paid to this pertinent question. 'Of course the Germans can't possibly win,' my father resumed rather portentously, 'because their troops have got no goloshes.' I was impressed by the profundity of this observation since I had never before heard of goloshes, the meaning of which had to be explained to me. My mother at the far end of the table looked up and said to my father quizzically, 'Hush! You'd better be careful not to put into their heads the idea of getting some, in case they should.' 'Should what?' he snapped. 'Win,' she answered. 'And this reminds me,' she turned her languid blue eyes in my direction, 'if you must go fishing in the pond, do get Nanny to put on your goloshes, or whatever it is you wear on these occasions.' It was this sentence which came as the shock to me, and is so particularly memorable, not the announcement of war, nor the deep significance of goloshes. My fishing, which had to do with Tobias, was, I innocently imagined, a deadly secret unknown so far to any human being but myself.

There used to hang in a passage of my grandmother's house a photogravure (after some well-known picture) in an Oxford frame of Tobias, a pretty, gentle and seraphic child, trailing a large fish. A dog gambolled ahead. Beside them tripped an angel with outspread wings, as it were protecting the boy. The angel was pointing to some distant object or goal outside the picture. This picture delighted and haunted me, just as the theme had inspired countless Renaissance artists, including Verocchio, Elsheimer, Domenichino and Rembrandt, to mention only those whose paintings of the subject can be seen in our National Gallery.

Now the story of Tobias, according to *The Peep of Day*, was briefly this. He had an old father called Tobit (who died shortly after the adventures about to be related, at the age of 158). Tobit, a man of exemplary piety, was most unfairly struck blind by sparrows dropping dirt (but according to the more candid Apocrypha, their excrement) into his eyes. Consequently he was unable to go on a long journey to look for a bag containing ten talents which he had mislaid. These misfortunes were entirely due to the malevolence of someone called Satan. The old man's son Tobias, who was possessed of every filial virtue, volunteered to retrieve the money and find a cure for Tobit's blindness. He enlisted the help of a companion who turned out to be the archangel Raphael. The two set off on their journey. Certain adventures, glossed over by *The Peep of Day* as being presumably in questionable taste, were, I discovered later from the Book of Tobit, concerned with a young lady called Sara, who had had seven husbands, each mysteriously killed on the wedding night, not apparently by her, but by Satan. This Satan has to be disposed of. The means of doing so is strangely chosen. While bathing Tobias is attacked by a large fish. Raphael helps him catch it. They open it and take out the heart, liver and gall. They presumably cook, for they certainly eat the remains of the fish. With the smoke from the heart and liver they drive away

Satan. Raphael discovers the bag of talents. The two youths return to Tobit. Tobias thereupon anoints with the gall of the fish his father's eyes which straightaway recover their sight. They all live happily ever after.

The picture with which I was familiar showed Tobias after the bathe and catch of the fish, at the early stage of his journey, when he was moved by the holy intention of slaying the devil who had blinded Tobit, stolen his money and in other ways upset God. As I have already indicated I saw myself in the summer of 1914 as Tobias, and in accordance with usual practice during my illusions it behoved me to enact his rôle. In the first place I had, like Tobias, my dog. He was a white bull terrier, called Tyke, a great blustering, extrovert dog, and my inseparable companion. Although originally my father's property, Tyke soon attached himself to me, as I attached myself to him. We confided in one another, consulted one another, conspired together, teased, abused, praised and consoled each other. We talked together incessantly. We shared each other's food, bed, and basket. All the same Tyke thought me ridiculously squeamish and over-scrupulous about certain matters. For instance, when I cuffed him for lifting his leg against the curtains, he growled; and when I admonished him for regurgitating in front of women, he looked hurt. I thought him greedy and often tactless. If I were trying to hide under the sofa when called to bed, he would as often as not give me away by loudly gnawing his bone, or yawning like a train going through a tunnel. Nevertheless we had a deep understanding, and I can truthfully say that Tyke's love for me was wonderful, passing the love of women.

In the second place I had my Raphael, and in the third place was to have my fish, as we shall shortly see. There were other analogies between my circumstances and Tobias's. I too had an aged father (he was then thirty-four) who was blind (in one eye through an accident at polo). That he might have mislaid a bag of talents was easily reconcilable with fact, for he was constantly losing money at poker and racing. The stage was all set for the story to be re-enacted. Unfortunately events did not turn out quite as they should. Dog and fish gave me away. Raphael was to prove the first of my disillusions with a superior being.

The immediate problem was how to catch a fish. I had already made several vain attempts at the shallow end of the great pond with a worm on a pin, bent and tied to a piece of string. One of these attempts had evidently been witnessed by my mother. All met with failure. In any event the only fish likely to be caught by this means were roach and perch, which were far too small for my purpose. *The Peep* said that Tobias had bathed and been attacked by his fish. But I was terrified of bathing ever since I nearly drowned while being taught to swim. My father with this laudable objective in view had rigged up a belt, which, attached round my stomach, he suspended by means of a pole from the bank. Choosing the deepest end of the pond he thus held me in the water, and instructed me how to manipulate my arms and legs. During the lesson a telegram was brought to him about a race which he had either won or lost. Having slowly read it through and written out a reply, which he handed to Goddard, our parlour-maid, he redirected his attentions to me. By this time I was invisible, floundering in several feet of mud at the bottom of the pond. Only a few faint bubbles revealed my whereabouts. For years after this experience I could not face the prospect of being on or, far worse, being in the water.

It is now that Raphael enters the scene in the shape of Colley, one of Mrs Hartwell's grandsons. He was very much my senior in years and worldly wisdom, but, as was not unusual with village children in those days, of sadly stunted growth. Indeed he may have been twelve or more, yet was scarcely any taller than I. Colley had short-cut, carroty hair, which stood bolt upright whenever he removed his cloth cap. His wicked little face was covered with freckles, and his nose perpetually running. He wore a Norfolk jacket, pepper-and-salt knickerbockers, and boots with no laces where laces ought to have been. I did not particularly care for him; and I am sure he despised me. But – and this is the awful thing – it was in his interest to be fairly nice to me, because I could in return for favours give him presents, either toys with which I had got bored, cakes which I scrounged from the kitchen, or even occasional pennies out of my pocket money. The great advantage of Colley was that he recognized no obstacles. He invariably found a way round difficulties, a way out of scrapes, and he was adept at making with his hands from nothing whatever was needed in an emergency. He was also always ready to listen and fall in with an adventure, however preposterous it may have seemed to him. What he really felt about it he kept tightly to himself.

I must, I said to Colley, have a fish, a very large fish, and I then explained to him the reason why. He listened silently, and expressed no astonishment. He showed no overt sympathy with my determination to exorcize Satan, but his eyes glistened when I mentioned the need to recover Tobit's money. At last he said slowly that everything I asked for could be done; and that he was willing to be my guide throughout. To my delight too he did not stipulate for any immediate *quid pro quo*. Then he reminded me that there were in the pond some immensely large, immensely ancient carp, even more ancient than Tobit. They were greatly venerated by my father who claimed that they or their ancestors had originally been stocked in the pond by the monks, whose property the place had been before the Reformation. If ever accidentally caught by a guest they had to be thrown back into the water immediately. In truth they seldom were caught owing to their extraordinary intelligence.

> 'Of all the fish that swim the watery mead,
> Not one in cunning can the carp exceed.'

was probably the only couplet my father knew by heart. He frequently quoted it, always adding that it came from the Badminton Library volume on Angling.

One afternoon when my parents were out the deed was done by the ingenious method of frightening a shoal of fish with a gong and driving them into a net stretched across a corner of the pond. With much adroitness Colley selected the fattest and most venerable carp, which he killed by bashing it on the head with a stone. The sight of the great golden brown body with its sulky mouth and drooping moustache laid on the grass made me feel an accomplice in a gross act of patricide. But this was no occasion for indulging in guilt. Colley threaded a string through the creature's gills, and together we hid the corpse in the bushes.

The next step preparatory to the recovery of my father's money and sight was to exorcize Satan in a way best calculated to please God. Colley and I agreed that whereas God was omnipresent at all times of the day and night, Satan only vouchsafed his presence during church services. I daresay this theory is strictly speaking heretical, but we knew no better. Unfortunately our church was the lesser of two in the parish, and services were not necessarily held in it every Sunday morning. I rather think the next service came quite ten days after we caught the carp. Certainly it was Evensong at six o'clock, just before my usual bedtime. My sister, brother and I never attended this service, and were taken to church only in the mornings.

By half-past five on this particular Sunday Tyke and I took advantage of the normal free half-hour between coming down to the drawing-room during the grown-up's tea and my bed-time. Five to 5.30 was the worst half hour of the day. Apart from breakfast it was the only time of the day I ever saw my father. He was terribly bored by the interview which he felt duty-bound to grant. I would be spruced up in the nursery, led to the drawing-room by Nanny, and pushed by her through the door which then closed softly behind me. I felt like a nervous actor stepping on to the stage, uncertain of his part and lines, and made more nervous by the uncertainty how Tyke, who always slipped in with me, was going to behave. For he was sure either, in an access of tail wagging, to knock from a saucer a scalding cup of tea into my father's lap, or to dribble on the carpet in anticipation of chocolate cake. In fact on weekdays when there were no visitors staying, I was an actor, and the drawing room was my stage. My parents would be sitting in silence, munching thin slices of bread and butter. 'Come in!' my mother would call with unconvincing cheeriness, and I would shyly advance. 'And what are you going to recite to us today, darling?' she would ask kindly. Rehearsed by Nanny with whom repetition never palled, I would reply overbrightly, 'Sandy Hill.' 'Oh God, not again!' my father would moan, picking up the *Morning Post*, his refuge on every awkward occasion, and retreating into the sporting news. Abashed by this reaction, and hesitant, I would nevertheless begin:

'When I went up Sandy-hill
I met a sandy-boy;
I cut his throat, I sucked his blood
And left his skin –
And left his skin –' I repeated

'A –', prompted my mother, 'a hang –'. 'A hanging-o', I exclaimed, relieved but dissatisfied with myself as well I needed to be. I seldom got any further. My father seldom emerged from the *Morning Post* unless it was to say with immense relief, 'Good night! Sleep tight! And mind the fleas don't bite!' With these valedictory words the interview was over for another twenty-four hours.

Soon after half-past five this Sunday afternoon Tyke and I were trotting across the lawn unobserved through the drawn sunblinds to keep a tryst with Colley. It had been a transcendentally hot day. The grass was parched brown and the worm casts felt like wire beneath my bare feet. By arrangement Colley was to be at the door in the wall beside the pigeon-house, which gave access to the garden from the village green. I lifted the latch and let him in. Tyke gave a great yelp and bound of welcome which nearly knocked him over. 'Now shut up, Tyke!' I shouted, 'and behave yourself. No noise,' and I gave a lunge with my leg, which missed him and sent me sprawling on the grass. This was Tyke's opportunity to jump on me and lick my face. I picked myself up and assumed the composure required by the solemnity of the ritual now to be observed. There was little difficulty in locating the carp. Tyke made a bee-line for it among the bushes. I regret to say that because of the weather we had been having that August, it was horribly high, a factor I had not taken into account. Gingerly I picked up the string threaded through the carp's gills. Slowly I trailed the fish towards the church, Tyke alternately sniffing it with interest and bounding ahead, and Colley walking beside me. The procession crossed the lawn, skirted the rock garden, passed the north side of the house and continued down the short length of drive leading to the churchyard gate. Tyke and Colley were behaving with exemplary reverence, while I took great pains to adopt the seraphic air of Tobias in my grandmother's photogravure.

Into the churchyard we went and from the church porch descended two steps into the nave. I knew that Mrs Hartwell never came to ring the bell before 5.45, although she was seldom later. We therefore had only a few minutes for the initial ceremony. We walked in orderly fashion into the chancel, stopping at the altar rails. We pushed open the stiff gate and passed through. I laid the carp on a black marble tomb slab. Colley whipped out of his knickerbockers a large, bone-handled knife, and in a flash slid a blade down the creature's belly. With that accompanying instrument, which every schoolboy's knife used to contain, a sort of hook ostensibly for taking stones out of horses' hooves, Colley ripped out the soggy entrails, which he scooped into the brass alms dish on the altar. The stink was more revolting than any I have ever smelled since. Gritting my teeth and trying not to vomit because my turn to officiate was now come, I took the alms dish, raised it above my head, as I had seen the Vicar do, and uttered an incantation calculated to denounce Satan and all his works. I waited. Nothing happened. Then from the gravel path outside I heard a distant shuffling. 'Quick!' said Colley, 'It's Gran.' He seized the alms dish from me and banged it, with its contents, on the altar. A brassy cacophony echoed round the empty church. Immediately a cloud of bats – or were they sparrows? – rose from behind the monuments against the north wall, circled and wheeled out of the west door. 'The fish!' I exclaimed, rather awed and anxious. Colley picked up the gutted carcase by the tail and dangling the ghastly object under my nose, said with a leer, 'You are meant to eat this.' I gave an ugly retch. By now Mrs Hartwell was in the porch. With much presence of mind Colley quickly thrust the remains of the carp behind the harmonium. 'Follow me,' he said. Dragging Tyke by the collar the two of us ducked under the altar cloth. There we were obliged to remain for more than half an hour.

Colley and I enjoyed an excellent view of the Evensong service through the altar fringe which hung just below the needlework text, 'Blessed are the pure in heart'. We watched Mr Swift on the corkscrew music stool – sometimes the seat came right off during the voluntary when my sister remembered before service to unscrew it far enough – bent over the harmonium. Normally no emotions were registered on that pale, impassive face gazing either at the keyboard or at the sky through the lancet window. But this evening the pallor turned to a dirty green, the nostrils dilated and quivered, and the drooping mouth had flecks of foam at the corner which was exposed to our view. I thought Mr Swift was going to be sick. Gallantly he held his ground. Emily Empey however got up and left the chancel. The schoolmistress sat with a handkerchief stuffed into her mouth, and sang not a note. Even Colley, whose senses were not acute, whispered to me, 'Nice stench, ain't it?' The only one who did not object, rather who positively relished it, was Tyke. In spite of my hand across his muzzle he began whimpering and, as usual, dribbling. I tapped him severely on the forehead. His response was to wag his tail, which had got outside the altar cloth and thump it violently against the marble floor. Mr Swift, his hands poised over the keys, but by now quite incapable of playing an Amen, or indeed a chord of any sort, turned a glazed eye in our direction. Tyke struggled with me, slipped his collar and let out a yell of expectancy. In one bound he had leapt the altar rails and bolted behind the harmonium, where he fell upon the mutilated carp. Clutching the unwholesome object in his teeth, tossing his head and sneezing with satisfaction, he stalked down the nave. On the porch mat he proceeded to have a delicious meal. The stink, which until then had been more or less confined to the chancel, was thus evenly distributed over the whole church.

In my hiding place I felt very put out since nothing like this incident had been recorded in the *Peep of Day* version of the Book of Tobit. My father too was clearly displeased, for he went and chased Tyke into the churchyard. Meanwhile those members of the congregation who were not too nauseated began singing the last hymn, unaccompanied. My father returned scowling to hand round the collection bag. At the same time the Vicar left the pulpit and made for the altar.

Being ostensibly Broad rather than Low – he would, I feel sure, have been flagrantly High, but for my father – the Vicar indulged, whenever possible, in 'antics'. One of these was to prostrate himself in front of the altar, his manipled arms outstretched, for all the world like a specimen butterfly with a pin through its thorax. To my embarrassment I found his grey head within an inch or two of my hand. I could easily have tickled it, or tweaked out a hair. Hearing my father approach the chancel he rose and, as was his wont, picked up the alms dish – still apparently unaware of what it contained – on which to receive the oblations, preparatory to blessing them. Desperately I realized that the Tobias ritual was going awry. So raising the altar cloth I crept out. 'No, no, no!' I shouted with all the strength of my six years. Horror-struck the Vicar put down the alms dish on one end of the altar. My father, no less appalled, dumped the collection bag on the other. I on the contrary was not to be deflected from enacting my culminating rôle, strictly in accordance with the version in *The Peep*, which had been read to me time and again. I even knew by heart the words describing this supreme moment: 'And Tobias ran unto his father, taking hold of him; and he strake of the gall on his father's eyes, saying Be of good hope, Tobit.'

Inversely however, my father tried to take hold of me. But he did not succeed before I plunged both hands into the alms dish and began, while he was still bending down, to smear his glass eye with the carp's stinking entrails, and utter another suitable incantation. In return for these benefactions my father let out a growl of ingratitude and disgust, and firmly grasped me round the waist. Having apologized to the Vicar – for he could do no less – he marched off with me loudly protesting and vainly kicking under his arm.

During the skirmish I just detected Colley's frayed sleeve emerge from one end of the altar cloth, and his grubby little hand deftly seize the collection bag. From the gesture I knew that Tobit was never going to recover his talents. Raphael had truly played his part better than Tobias.

II

SHE

THE WAR was still on; by which I mean the 1914 War, although the incident I am about to relate did not take place in that year. On the contrary it was the summer of 1917 when there were still to run several more months of hell and anguish for my parents' generation. After that, as everyone then knew, peace would be restored for ever and England would return to its contented, pastoral, sleepy beauty of sun-drenched lawns, with tea under the lime trees from silver kettles served by smiling parlour-maids in print dresses, bows and caps.

This dream was as yet unrealized when my parents arranged for me to go to school. It was, they decided, high time, for I was already well over eight years old. Convention demanded that little boys should be wrenched from home at this age, and dumped amongst a hundred others in a grim institution as unlike home as could be devised. Besides, by the middle of the War the even tenor of my home had been very much disturbed. My father who because of his one eye was disabled from fighting – much to his distress – was intensively farming for King and country, and my mother, whenever she could foist us children upon my grandmother, or some obliging relation, was nursing the wounded, cherishing Belgian refugees, licking up envelopes, distributing comforters, or hoeing the soil. She took these duties far more seriously than they took her. Pampered, flighty, and susceptible to whatever wind was blowing, she was quite incapable of sustained hard labour, or of sticking to the same job for a longer period than, at most, three months. At the end of it she would move to another job, not out of dissatisfaction or disillusion, but because she genuinely felt called 'to do her bit' for England through some different medium more suited to her peculiar talents. So she shifted like quicksilver in a barometer, exasperating her employers, charming her colleagues, trying most desperately, failing most delightfully, loved and forgiven by all.

During one of these interludes my busy mother decided that she could spare a day to introduce me to my preparatory school. It never occurred to her – and my absent father was too preoccupied with his asparagus beds to give advice – that schools prefer little boys, especially new boys, to join at the beginning of term. I doubt whether she would have comprehended had it been explained to her, but I daresay, so tender-hearted was she, that she might conceivably have been influenced by a plea – had there been any one to make it – that it was kinder to the child, quite apart from being more convenient for the authorities. Had I at the time realized the predicament I feel sure I could easily have persuaded her. As it was, my mother gave notice to the Evesham Cottage Hospital at 6.30 p.m. on 3rd June that she was leaving that evening for good, and would be taking up the duty of assistant sorting officer at the Post Office at 6 a.m. on 5th June. Whether the Post Office was fully cognizant of its impending privilege is beside the point. The indirect consequences of this quixotic behaviour were disastrous to my happiness at my preparatory school for the ensuing three or four years that I remained there, until indeed I went on to Eton, where the manner of my previous initiation was unknown.

I adored my mother. In my eyes she was beautiful, attractive, romantic and amusing. Her sense of the ludicrous and her utter indifference to the proprieties never failed to stimulate me. It was only later that I sometimes became embarrassed by her irrational conduct and her sentimentality, which I discovered to be a trifle insincere. In those days the scales had not fallen from my admiring eyes. The only snag to our happy relationship was that I knew myself to be a disappointment to her. I simply could not respond to her rapidly shifting ambitions that I should become, when I grew up, a balloonist, an explorer of the Malaysian jungle or of the Antarctic (the two places were indeterminate), a Master of Fox Hounds, a submarine diver and lastly a 'reincarnation' as she put it of the Scarlet Pimpernel, who, it clearly did not occur to her, had never been exactly incarnate in the first instance. For to be candid, I was a cissy child. I did not favour any of the careers she planned for me. I was consistent in my longing to become Rouge Dragon Pursuivant and spend my days in comfortable surroundings manufacturing for myself a totally fictitious but noble ancestry deriving from some Knight of the Round Table. I had the sense to cherish this ambition tight within my bosom. My mother, who had no sense of history and was totally un-snobbish, would have been horrified.

By 7 o'clock that evening a crunching on the gravel drive outside the nursery window announced that my mother had returned. To the terror of the neighbourhood she had taught herself to drive after my father and Haines had enlisted and gone off to the agricultural and military fronts. The Minerva landaulette, with its Bedford cord upholstery, two 'strapontins', veneered mahogany shelves for calling-cards, smelling-salt bottle and handmirror, and its netted bulb with speaking tube, was jacked high under dust-sheets in the motor-house. My mother had somehow acquired as more suited to the times a second-hand Ford dray, known as a Tin Lizzie, very high off the ground, with a snub-nose bonnet of which the radiator cap shook in a peculiarly menacing fashion when the machine was in motion. As far as I remember the chief advantage of this make of vehicle lay in its much vaunted simplicity of drive. There were no brake or gear levers, and only two pedals. A slight complication lay in knowing how to manipulate that pedal which was not the brake. According to the pressure the machine responded in different ways. If you pressed once gently the vehicle went forward in bottom gear, until you pressed it twice gently when it proceeded in second gear, and so on several times until top gear was reached. If you pressed sharply it would go immediately into reverse. Now my mother being an impatient woman would start off with one and possibly two gentle pressures of the pedal. But she could seldom keep this treatment up five or six times in succession. When she had reached a roaring 30 miles an hour on the flat preparatory to slipping into top gear, she would habitually give a violent pressure with the foot. The inevitable consequence was terrible to witness. The machine bellowed, shook like a dog with a rat, threw all the luggage off the dray, and ground angrily to a halt. The extraordinary thing was that in spite of being slipped straight from fifth gear into reverse it bore no lasting resentment. After ten minutes' cranking by an obliging passer-by it would start up again (not for worlds, and quite rightly, would my mother consider winding it herself ever since she had heard of a woman breaking most of her fingers and both wrists in the attempt).

As I was saying, at 7 o'clock on 3rd June 1917 the Tin Lizzie stopped with an ugly jerk outside our front door. I watched my mother step with great agility on to the running board and jump to the ground. I see her now elegant in the tight-fitting V.A.D. uniform which she was about to discard, doubtless in favour of the day-after-tomorrow's equally well tailored G.P.O. coat and skirt. She smiled triumphantly up to the nursery window and held aloft a rather battered pheasant which she had just killed on the road. It was, she exclaimed, most providential, and she would pack it in my tuck-box for tomorrow. This was literally the first intimation I received of my impending fate. I then noticed that the dray, which had been empty when she left in the morning, was groaning with packages of the most luxurious sort – bundles of asparagus, chips of strawberries, boxes of Huntley & Palmer biscuits, baskets of cakes, cartons of cream and pots of Gentleman's Relish, to mention only a few of the delicacies on board. They had, my mother affirmed with an angelic expression, been presented by friends anxious to make her little boy's first term a resounding success. I had a nasty suspicion that some at any rate had been given by the Evesham shopkeepers under quite different impressions, for it was well known that my mother was, on top of her exacting war work, organizing charity drives of various kinds, including a 'blow-out' in our garden the following Sunday for the children of Belgian refugees.

While I helped unload the dray my mother explained how, thanks to the beneficence of the Cottage Hospital and the Post Office, both of which had graciously allowed her twenty-four hours' leave for the purpose, she could spare all the next day taking me to Upland House. Miserable though she was to part with me she felt absolutely confident that I would be happy there because the house had once belonged to the de Frevilles and they had simply loved it. Neither she nor I questioned that conditions at Upland House, now a boys' boarding school in the third year of the bloodiest war in history, could be different from those pertaining to the de Freville ownership in its Edwardian heyday.

Fortified by these assurances I watched the preparation of two dome-lidded but battered servants' trunks, with layers of internal trays (considered quite good enough for school), two gladstone bags, a hat-box for the 'topper' obligatory on Sunday church parades, and the indispensable play-box and tuck-box. Every boy, I was told, had to have a tuck-box. Into the trunks were packed quantities of suits, jerseys, shirts and underclothes – I still have a vision of thick woollen combinations large enough for a prize-fighter, being squeezed on top. Not one of these garments had I even tried on. The whole lot had been collected over the years in preparation for this moment, from the discarded wardrobe of various teenage cousins now grown up and themselves serving in the trenches. The delicacies, already mentioned, were duly packed in the wooden and iron-clad tuck-box. So abundant were they that the lid could not be made to shut properly, and had to be secured by odd pieces of string tied together in a concatenation of 'granny' knots.

Early the following morning we set off. Leaving home was heart-rending. My natural lack of self-confidence was not mitigated by the strange garments I was obliged to wear for the first time in my life. To begin with I had – like the proverbial slum children of those

days – never before worn socks or shoes. It had been one of my
mother's tenets that such impedimenta were bad for growing feet.
The result was that mine were hard as iron, impervious to wounds
and cuts, and perfectly all right so long as they were not encum-
bered. But the moment they found themselves imprisoned in wool
and stiff leather they practically ceased to function. I can scarcely
believe the particular boots I was forced into on this occasion were
too small, when I recall how grotesquely oversize was everything
else I was made to wear. Whether too small or too large, they were
absolute agony, and I could move only with the greatest difficulty.
To add to the trouble my adolescent cousin's trousers were far too
big. The legs trailed over my feet and behind the ankles like
bedraggled hose pipes. I must have looked like some ghastly carica-
ture of a dwarf hobbling on amputated stumps. Besides, no amount
of pulling at the belt with its snake buckle would keep the beastly
things up. This could only be achieved by me never letting go of the
waist. The moment I did so, down they would fall, literally to the
ground. Furthermore, for the first time in my life – I was, let me
remind you, eight – I was obliged to wear a shirt with starched cuffs
and collar, tie and waistcoat. Now in the summer months I had
been accustomed to wear nothing beyond the briefest pair of
shorts. In the winter an additional flimsy jersey was the utmost
concession granted. My mother's admiration of Captain Scott of
the Antarctic was unbounded, and she had read and approved his
dying instructions to his widow to bring up their son, Peter, in the
hard way. In Peter Scott's case these directions were, I am the first
to admit, amply justified. In my own, either because I was not born
in the heroic mould, or because of the unnaturally abrupt manner
in which I was changed overnight from a potential Tarzan of the
Apes into a pantomime clown, they were not. The shame of the
transformation effected on 4th June 1917 has never left me. I have
been horribly clothes-conscious ever since.

My mother on the other hand was dressed to kill. Our journey
necessitated passing through London, which in those days meant
for every country lady putting on her best clothes, even though all

that the capital might see of her was through the windows of a taxi-cab driving from Paddington to Euston and back again. What precisely she had on I do not remember, beyond a long, full dress of some pale, diaphanous material ending just above her beautifully shaped ankles, and a large straw hat, rather high in the crown, with a wide floppy brim. There were ribbons in it, I fancy, matching others about her dress. Although mourning the death in action of several friends during the past fearful months and soon to be grief-stricken by that of her brother in battle, she was not one to indulge in ostensible weeds.

A strange pair we must have seemed climbing into the Tin Lizzie. I was so numbed by my unaccustomed situation that I did not respond as affectionately as I should have done to the embraces of my sister, brother, and the maids assembled to wave us off. Besides I felt so sick with journey pride that I dared not open my mouth. I had never before set foot outside Worcestershire, and now I was about to hobble, there was no other word for it, across the threshold into the great hostile unknown. The luggage was on board, seven pieces in all, whereas I was soon to learn it was customary for little boys to manage with, at very most, two. An obliging villager had been mobilized to crank the machine, the operation of which involved a series of appalling kicks accompanied by back-fires and the winding handle shooting into the air. After a dozen or more turns the engine at last condescended to snort, stagger, shake and then roar. Having reversed once through the front door and twice into the herbaceous border, the Ford dray bolted down the drive, through the gates and into the village street, scattering clouds of gravel and dust in all directions.

We reached Evesham station without misadventure. All the porters from this small market town had long ago been called up. Luckily the Member of Parliament for our division happened to be travelling to London with his wife and, I think, the First Lord of the Admiralty, on the same train. Without the slightest compunction my mother organized a relay of these three august and correct personages to stagger with my domed trunks, gladstone bags, play-, tuck- and hat-boxes across the lines to the far platform. I can see now Mrs Eyres Monsell bejewelled, Ascoty and holding a pair of lorgnettes in one hand, making a token gesture with very ill grace of dragging, with the First Lord's assistance, the tuck-box across the railway sleepers, while my mother on the far side shouted directions and warnings that the through express to Worcester was due at any moment. When our 'up' train drew in the problem of how to lift the luggage into the van was far simpler. There were plenty of passengers consisting of wounded soldiers and men too old to be serving, who were more than anxious to oblige us. The Eyres Monsells and the First Lord had mysteriously disappeared to the far end of the platform.

This was the first time I had ever been inside a train. Excursions to my grandmother's house in the north of the county, which were the only journeys I had yet experienced, had been made by road. I was thrilled but not a little alarmed. The prospect of arrival at Paddington, the bustle and noise of a terminus and the awful probability of there again being no porters was disturbing. Moreover I dreaded being told to button-hole the Prime Minister or the Archbishop of Canterbury, and order him to lift without argument my luggage into a taxi.

As it happened there was no need, for at Paddington the train slowly drew up alongside a phalanx of female porters of most formidable aspect. They were, I think, wearing trousers. Certainly they wore short jackets very tightly buttoned across the bust. This made them bulge in unexpected places and appear extremely unwomanly. They had fuzzy hair pulled over shiny cheeks from under workmen's cloth caps. Even my mother was shocked and hailed them with, for her, unwonted asperity. They on their side were clearly shocked by her holiday appearance, dressed as she was in her smartest clothes – an unfair judgment considering that this was probably her first day off duty since August 1914, if taking me to school could exactly be described as a treat. My mother need not have wasted her breath, for the monstrous regiment paid no attention to her, but precipitated themselves upon the soldiers. I was surprised how indifferent the soldiers were to their attentions, and wondered why they preferred to shoulder their kit-bags when others were offering to do it for them. It was only after waiting for the Amazons' return to our platform that we managed to bribe one of them reluctantly to fetch us a trolley.

The impression London made upon me as we drove across it bolt upright in a high-roofed taxi with large windows is not very distinct. It seemed incredibly large and incredibly ancient. I do not suppose that the squares and crescents on our way to Euston station contained more than a dozen buildings of later date than the Regency. There was hardly any traffic and our taxi kept to the crown of the cambered, cobbled streets. I can hear to this day the soothing purr of the metal studs in the tyres as we sped along. It was however interrupted by the driver ceaselessly pressing a fat, rubber horn like a ball-cock attached to a brass serpent, which undulated over the right mudguard. The noise emitted was disappointing – the thin chirrup of an insolent sparrow. My other strong memory is of a deliciously sweet smell of petrol fumes, mingled with that of horse droppings and antirrhinums.

The unloading of our luggage from the taxi to the train passed without incident. I rather think we obliged a postman to stagger under the load, which must have taken him at least two shifts. For my mother refused to discriminate between one uniform and another. Anyone under a peaked cap – and the more gold braid the more peremptory it made her – was a railway porter, if that is what she was wanting at the time. If she happened to be thinking of affairs of state she was apt to make a similar mistake, in reverse as it were. A year or so later I recall her addressing the hall porter at Brown's Hotel with the words: 'Well, Field Marshal, and how is the Peace Conference getting on?'

We were soon comfortably ensconced in a first-class carriage with twenty minutes to spare before the train was scheduled to leave. By this time I had worked up a bit of an appetite. My mother thereupon took the opportunity of preparing our picnic luncheon. The contents of a basket which she had been carrying, were spread upon both seats, and a methylated spirit lamp was balanced precariously upon the empty upturned basket. This was lit and applied to a Cona coffee machine. On no account, she explained, must the lamp be allowed to burn while the train was running, or the whole apparatus might explode. Such a thing had been known to happen even when a train was stationary. As I was a nervous child the warning slightly alarmed me. Then an unfortunate thing happened. My mother got bored.

This was by no means an unusual state of affairs with her. But I secretly wished she had not chosen this moment to leave the carriage in search of a newspaper. I was left alone with the methylated spirit lamp and a vast globe of glass, at the bottom of which a few drops of discoloured liquid began angrily to bubble, while up a tube gushed a fountain into a steaming cylinder of coffee grounds. While I watched, fascinated and impotent, the carriage gave a lurch, and the train drew out of Euston station. I dashed to the window, vainly scanning the crowded platform for my mother. There was not a vestige of her to be seen, and we plunged into a tunnel.

I was panic-stricken. Here I was alone for the first time in my life, in a train, bound for I knew not where. Like an idiot I had not had the curiosity or the gumption to enquire the name of the station we were booked for. As for the name of the school, that had escaped me. Going through a tunnel can at the best of times be an alarming experience. For the first time in a child's life it can be his idea of hell. A stifling, sulphurous smoke soon filled the compartment, while outside a roar of wheels was accompanied by sparks. The carriage however was not pitch dark, for on the picnic basket the blue flame from the methylated spirit lamp was wrapping itself round the empty bowl in a perfect frenzy of rage. Clearly the explosion and an end to existence were imminent. What was to be done? I adopted the only course available to me. I lost my head and, clutching my waist and tripping over my trouser legs, ran bellowing down the corridor.

The first thing that ought to be inculcated into children is that grown-ups of every age and every country are invariably nice to

34

them when *in extremis*. They are seldom very nice to each other, and not always nice to children who have nothing the matter with them. But in order to melt the stoniest adult heart a child, howsoever unattractive and displeasing, has merely to appear slightly out of sorts. Thereupon the gruffest old maid and the most dyspeptic old colonel will instantly drop her knitting and his *Times* newspaper, and rush headlong to its support. I was unaware of this simple truth when I made a frightful hullabaloo in the first-class corridor of the 12.52 from Euston that day. Mercifully I soon found myself in the enormous hot bosom of a surprised lady passenger, who without hesitation administered succour and comfort. Through my tears I feebly pointed in the direction I had come from. It was as well that I did so. The lady's companion, hearing a deafening report, dashed to my compartment where the glass bulb, having indeed exploded in a thousand fragments, had not extinguished the spirit lamp which continued to blaze merrily. With great presence of mind the heroic companion hurled it out of the window.

Once I had recovered my composure I was bombarded with questions. What on earth was I doing by myself boiling water on a wicker basket in a railway train? Who was I? And where was I going? To the last question I was unable to give a satisfactory reply. To a school, I answered, to a large school of over 100 boys. Had anyone a notion where such a school was to be found? Or at what station I ought to get out? My new friends were at first nonplussed. They suggested at length that my wisest course would be to disembark at the next stop, which was Hemel Hempstead, and put my implicit trust in the station master. He would no doubt eventually establish my identity and possibly my ultimate destination. I fell in with this sensible proposition.

At Hemel Hempstead the train drew up. I got out, and my kind friends lowered the seven pieces of luggage, plus the picnic basket on to the platform. Before I had time to collect my wits and wave them goodbye, the train chugged off. I did not have long to look around. Suddenly a familiar voice screamed out my name, and there, running towards me was, of all people, my mother. To my surprise she was in a most extraordinary state of disorderliness and dirt. She had lost her hat, there were smuts on her face and hair, and her pretty dress was crumpled and covered with oil stains. My joy and relief were so great, however, that it never occurred to me to criticize her behaviour, which was at once explained in a breathless volley of excitement. On leaving the carriage at Euston she had failed to find a newspaper stall and, instead, had got into conversation with the engine driver, the most charming, the most sympathetic engine driver that ever was born. He had begged her to get into his cabin so that he might show her the most marvellous brass gadgets, all brightly polished and so clean you could see your reflection in them. Before she knew what was happening the whistle had blown and they were off. One of her life's ambitions was now fulfilled. She knew I would understand and not mind. Had the station master seen? And if so, would he arrest her? How clever I had been to get out at Hemel Hempstead and not get carried on to Crewe, or wherever the next stop was. She was ravenous. Had I eaten all the sandwiches and drunk all the coffee?

Having repaired the ravages of the fireman's cabin as best we could in the Ladies' Waiting Room with my handkerchief and spit, we considered how to proceed to Upland House. There was only one available means of doing this, namely by waking up an old cabby with a long drooping moustache, asleep on the box of a solitary vehicle in the station yard. Never can quite such an antiquated and dilapidated equipage have plied for hire. The old man nodding in the sun was roused after much prodding with my mother's parasol. Throughout the ensuing journey he never uttered a word, and may for all we knew to the contrary have been deaf and dumb. My mother took an instant dislike to him, declaring not without foresight that his lack of cooperation was calculated. He was no doubt a sad contrast to the dashing engine driver with whom she had spent the last blissful half hour. On the other hand all her vacillating maternal instincts were aroused by his horse, which must have been quite as old as its master. A more pathetic wreck of a horse could hardly be imagined. For a long while my mother could not make up her mind whether she had the heart to disturb it on so hot an afternoon, or whether she should report its condition to the local branch of the R.S.P.C.A. The old cabby refused to vouchsafe one word's response to her solicitude as to whether or not it was strong enough to pull us. In the end our necessity forced a reluctant decision from her that we must take the risk.

The four-wheeler was all of a piece with driver and animal. The open hood was in tatters, the black leather upholstery torn and the horsehair stuffing bursting through the seams. The perilous floor boards were littered with straw. Into the boot of this vehicle the old cabby was finally bullied into bundling the luggage, all but the heavy tuck-box. This was put instead in the middle of the floor between my mother's and my feet.

Without paying the slightest heed to our directions and questions the cabby started off at a snail's pace. He let the reins dangle over the horse's withers, folded his arms and apparently went to sleep again. There are of course few more agreeable ways of spending a hot summer's afternoon than that of ambling in an open four-wheeler through the Home Counties. But on this occasion my mother's pleasure was lessened by anxiety as to where precisely we were heading for, and extreme irritation with our driver's insubordination; mine was entirely dispelled by a sudden access of home-sickness and downright misery. By the time we had wandered through the town and into a lane between water meadows my mother's emotions had subsided – quick to anger she was quicker still to sweetness – whereas mine were if anything accentuated. In sensing this state of affairs she tried by every means to cheer me up, giving vent to a parent's usual catalogue of platitudes. The happiest time of my life was now dawning. The term always went by in a flash. I would soon be making the friends of a lifetime. 'Which reminds me,' she added, in a rather portentous and uncharacteristic tone, 'your father would wish me to give you a little, just a little piece of advice. About life generally.' She paused, and then suddenly corrected herself. 'On the whole, it might be better if you

asked the headmaster to explain all about the disgusting side of it.'
And then half to herself and half aloud, she added, 'Not that I
myself have ever found it *exactly* that.'

I of course had not the faintest idea what she was talking about.
At that particular moment every side of life appeared to me so disgusting that no amount of explanation by all the headmasters in
England could possibly improve it. Life to me meant weeks,
months and even years of banishment from home. For the second
time that day I burst into uncontrollable sobs. This sound evidently had some ameliorative effect upon the cabby, because he
cracked his whip and for the first time the old horse broke into an
uncomfortable jog trot.

When I had slightly recovered I noticed that we were passing
through a rusty pair of open gates. Ahead stretched an uphill drive
lined with clumps of faded ponticums. At the end of it as though
barring the way to eternity straddled the vast red brick mausoleum
of my dying hopes, covered with Virginia creeper and fire escapes.
Out of the front door of this lugubrious edifice were streaming
dozens of grey flannelled, becapped midgets, dressed exactly alike,
carrying cricket bats and pads, interspersed with a few white-flannelled giants in striped jackets and straw boaters. As I learned
afterwards, the 4th of June happened to be a half-holiday, and the
exodus of boys and masters on to the playing field coincided with
our ill-fated arrival. The spectacle before us was now too much for
my tender-hearted mother. 'How hid-jus!' she exclaimed. 'How
perfectly hid-jus! How could the de Frevilles . . . ?' She gave an ill-
concealed gulp and a few silent tears blazed a trail down her faintly
rouged cheeks. The remark had an electrical effect upon the cabby.
He actually gave a snort and lashed the hollow flanks of the old
horse, which suddenly plunged into a lolloping canter just as we
were approaching the carriage sweep.

My mother and I, both now sobbing uncontrollably, were pitch-
forked by the unexpected jolt against the tuck-box. Instantly there
was a harsh sound of rending woodwork. The tuck-box gave a
wobble, then a lurch and disappeared through the floor boards,

which clattered to the ground, our feet with them. The noise was alarming, the spectacle exceedingly humiliating. The two of us, shocked beyond measure, had no alternative to running inside the carriage as fast as our legs could carry us. Any other course would have invited instant and perhaps fatal injury, for we would have been knocked down by the seat we had precipitately left and then been crushed by the axle or the wheels. But the faster we ran and the louder we shouted to that brute of a cabby, who never once so much as turned his head in our direction, the more the old horse took the bit between its teeth. Round and round the sweep we went, and over and over the remains of the tuck-box, of which the contents – for the lid and bottom had broken off with the fall – made a ghastly contusion on the drive. Strawberries, petits-beurres biscuits, asparagus, cream and pheasants' feathers were churned into the gravel by a succession of wheels, and human and equine feet. My mother had the presence of mind to seize me by the arm and pull me along with her, or I should inevitably have been lost. Just before we completed the fourth round of the sweep one of the white-flannelled giants managed to catch hold of the bridle and, by dint of being dragged several yards along the gravel to the absolute detriment of his immaculate ducks, brought the sweating horse to a standstill.

The scene witnessed by the entire school was indescribable. My mother was hauled from the wreckage in a fit of hysterical giggles. Her dress was torn to shreds and her long hair was down to her waist. My plight was even more pitiable. In the mêlée I had completely lost my trousers. In fact it was a mercy that they had come off truly and properly: a miracle that the trailing extremities had not got caught in the wheel spokes, and possibly squeezed or throttled me to death. The two of us were then stretched on the grass and restored by the matron with sal volatile. All this while the abominable cabby was bending over us, making demands in dumb show for his fare and reparation money for the damage to his victoria.

The final ignominy was having to explain who we were. It transpired that my mother had failed to notify the headmaster that we were coming that afternoon. And although in later years she strenuously denied it, I have often wondered whether she had ever entered me for the school in the first place, or merely assumed that the headmaster would welcome any stray child whose parents dropped in on the off chance. Welcome me, or rather accept me he did. The kindest thing he could have done would have been to send us both packing there and then. As it was, the boys who witnessed our arrival never allowed me to forget it.

III

HE

MY FATHER was a good and honourable man, which says a great deal in his favour. His friends loved him. His tenants respected him. And, what is strange, other people's children liked him. But his horizons were hidebound. His standards were not mine and we seldom agreed upon fundamental issues. Towards the end of his life he grew mellow, gentle and almost sweet. We then got on fairly well together through a mutual tolerance and because of a shared anxiety, than which nothing helps more to unite the most disparate elements. But we remained as oil and water. In spite of the polarity of our views I can honestly say that I hold his memory in tender affection. It was not altogether his fault that he hatched in his nest, instead of a falcon, a young cuckoo. He was bewildered and distressed by his fledgeling. I now feel genuinely sorry and reproach myself for much lack of sympathy and, worse still, much deliberate unkindness towards one whose chief failings – and they are venial enough – were lack of imagination and aggressive shyness.

Until I left the nest we were continually sparring. In our contests he as the older bird was able to peck harder. He invariably got the better of me except once, when the long-term victory was mine. From this engagement I emerged with flying, but perhaps somewhat tarnished colours.

The difference between us was as much biological as temperamental. My mother may have had a good deal to do with it, albeit unconsciously. She can hardly be blamed for creating me in her image, for it was always being pointed out how I took after her side of the family exclusively, and bore not the remotest resemblance to his. To begin with, this was not flattering to my father's self-esteem. It was certainly true physically. It was pretty true psychically. I inherited her vagueness (what my father called 'moronic behaviour'), her love of animals, sunsets and general prettinesses ('damned nonsense'), and her unfortunate incapacity for hard work and what is termed getting on with life ('utter lack of moral fibre'). 'What on earth d'you suppose you two would do, I would like to know, if you found yourselves alone on a desert island? In the Indian Ocean?' my father once yelled at us during a picnic. He was incensed by our inability to open a box of preserved fruits. 'Rot,' my mother answered with a timid little smile. 'It isn't,' he snapped back, misunderstanding her meaning. 'I asked what would you do?' To which she languidly repeated, 'Rot. We would just rot.'

Although they were often unhappy together, went their own ways and even separated from time to time, I suspect that my father was always in love with her, whereas she certainly was not with him. Since he had a patently jealous nature he resented her deep love for me, a love which he at times rightly considered super-erogatory. He may without careful analysis have felt it to be just slightly incestuous simply because she and I were so much alike. Indeed when I was seventeen and she thirty-seven we looked more like twins than son and mother. In the holidays we were insepara-ble, and would loaf around the garden arm in arm, exchanging con-fidences and giggling in a highly annoying manner. We were then on just the same level of mental development, which is not saying much. At any rate my father, sensing that there was something con-trary to nature in our resemblance and our intimacy (how absolutely wrong he was on the last point), loathed me biologically. It was an effort for him to be polite to me. My mere presence put up his hackles. Being a very normal man he felt overcome by nausea as though he saw in me the wife of his bosom transformed all of a sudden into a boy.

If my presence was pain and grief to him my shortcomings were an unspeakable affront. In his eyes they were utterly deplorable, and he never failed to deplore them loudly in private and in front of others. The consequence was of course inevitable. They became more and more pronounced as the years went by and my fear of him gave place to indifference. Poor man, he was so on the spot, so practical, so invariably right. I was so dreamy, so butter-fingered, so dependably wrong. When told to fetch a screw-driver from his workshop, I would forget before I got there and come back with a sledge hammer, if I remembered to come back at all. I could not mend an electric light switch. I did not know the difference between a carburettor and a crankshaft. I could not catch a ball, or tie my shoe laces. Worse still, I did not fulfil any of those elementary prerequisites of a gentleman. I could never shoot a sitting rabbit, and I once in desperation shot a sitting pheasant. My seat on a horse was like a grocer's, and I invariably headed foxes and ran amok among the hounds. And when I fell off, which happened constantly, I would bring down a string of riders with me. My father on the contrary was extraordinarily handy, and a deft and practised sportsman. Excellent plumber, electrician, motor mechanic and carpenter, he delighted in taking tools from the hands of workmen and showing them how the job should be properly done. Never idle, he spent days on end standing on lavatory seats fiddling with ball cocks, or lying on his back covered with oil in the motor-house: that is to say on those when he was not hunting, stalking, shooting or racing. Sport of all kinds was the *ne plus ultra* of his existence. The prowess of the horse constituted in his eyes the history of England's greatness. His memory for equine trivialities was prodigious. Without hesitating he would rattle off the names of every Derby winner since the beginning of time – Bend Or 1880, Minoru 1909 – and would recall how on Thursday 13th February, 1897 the Heythrop pack found at Gallipot at noon, ran for one hour, ten and a half minutes to Stow-on-the-Wold and then killed a vixen in Mrs Twistleton-Fiennes' rock garden. 'But', and he would continue with a very boring emphasis, as though what he was about to impart mattered, 'But, having blown a gale from the north-east all that morning, it came on to rain at ten minutes past three. So at a quarter to four I turned my horse's head for home.'

Art on the other hand was anathema to him. The very word had on him the effect of a red rag upon a bull. He turned puce in the face and fumed at the mere mention of it; and his deadliest, most offensive adjective was 'artistic'. It denoted decadence, disloyalty to the Crown, and unnatural vice. To be called artistic by him with a biting sneer used to make me shake like an aspen leaf. I really believe he would have expected any man but his son, thus described, to challenge him to a duel for the rankest insult.

His contempt for intellectuals was profound, and he had a healthy dread of my becoming one. Books of course were taboo. Consequently I could only read in the holidays by stealth. I spent hours at night with a torch under the bedclothes so that he should not see a light through the cracks of the door and catch me in the act. And no matter how carefully I hid my books before returning to school, he always nosed them out, like a detective on the scent of cannabis, and threw them into the stoke-hole furnace. Of all the authors of all the languages the one who got his goat most was luckless Shakespeare. I never learned the reason for this particular hate and can only assume that Shakespeare was the one author (apart from the editor of the Badminton Library) he had heard of. I tremble to think what he might have done had he realized that I frequently took Oscar Wilde to bed with me. I was much alarmed when it was reported to him that I had been seen at the Stratford-on-Avon theatre in Marie Corelli's box for a performance of *Much Ado about Nothing*. Mercifully he mistook her for Marie Tempest or Mae West (I forget which) who, he supposed, had kindly given me a ticket for some children's pantomime in which she was acting. Of poetry he had an absolute horror, and once warned me darkly that if ever I published a poem he would send me straight to the colonies with only £5 in my pocket. Had he but foreseen the future he would have had no cause for fear. Not a single poem of mine has ever been accepted by any editor of any magazine.

My Eton career was a worry to him. Indeed I did not excel either at games (this depressed him inordinately) or work (which mattered far less) in spite of my intellectual pretensions. But I read prodigiously, if indiscriminately, spending most of my spare time in the School Library devouring my way through the Victorian novelists and the romantic poets. 'Much learning doth make thee mad' was my father's constant jibe, 'and it won't get you anywhere, except a lunatic asylum.' It may not have got me prizes because I was an undisciplined, unacademic child. But it did win me a number of devoted friends with similar interests, friends with whom I spent blissful summer afternoons and evenings, idly floating on the river and discussing the merits of Thackeray and Meredith, Shelley and Swinburne. My father was accordingly convinced that I had got into the wrong set. This was, strictly speaking, not true. The set I had got firmly into was the right one, consisting of sensitive, intelligent boys with enquiring minds. Those of them who have survived World War II and the vicissitudes of middle age, are now what are called distinguished ornaments of society. The wrong set at Eton, when I was there, consisted of enchanting, unserious, raffish boys, whose parents were for the most part cosmopolitan and rich. I was intoxicated by their glamour, but never really accepted as one of them. This was not for lack of trying, but because I was in no sense grand or sophisticated enough to adorn their colourful company. Nevertheless my flirtation with them nearly got me into very hot water.

As I grew older I became increasingly bold and provocative. By parading an assumed dilettantism and aestheticism I gloried in taunting my wretched father. I wore my hair long when it was not considered effeminate to wear it short, and I favoured for a brief period outrageous Oxford bags, which swished voluptuously round the ankles during those abandoned evening strolls along Eton High Street. I took nothing very seriously except myself. At the age of seventeen I fell desperately in love.

There had drifted unexpectedly into our conventional family

orbit an exotic little cousin, called Jane Puleston. She was unlike any of the staid country relations to whom I was accustomed. And the only reason why she had descended upon our Worcestershire manor house was the impending break-up of her first marriage. She was momentarily at a loose end and in need of succour away from the lights and follies of Mayfair. My mother took pity on her and not without hesitation gave her a welcome. My grandmother, who took an instantaneous dislike to her, said she was fast. She was certainly extremely pretty, with a pouting, wistful little face like a kitten's, infinitely silly and, I now realize, rather pathetic. She could not have been the victim of any other decade than the Twenties, being rootless and blown willy-nilly like heedless thistle-down on every wind of pleasure. She was uncalculating, harmless and wretched. She was certainly seductive, wore very chic clothes, and was drenched in expensive Parisian scents. For the whole of the Christmas holidays of 1925–6 she stayed with us. Every morning she remained in bed, leafing French novelettes and combing her Pekingese's silky ears. In the afternoons she rolled her moon eyes at any man who happened to be about, not excluding the Vicar. She spoke in a special baby language of her own and referred to herself in the third person. In the end my mother and the servants were driven almost mad by her.

Her effect upon me was electric. In my wildest dreams I had not conjured up a being more intoxicating. The very smell of her drove me into ecstasies of excitement. I wrote her reams of atrocious verse which she professed to admire, and before the holidays were over imagined that she was in love with me. I returned to Eton a changed being. At the same time my mother managed to chase her back to London.

During the ensuing Easter half Janie used faithfully to come down from London to Eton on Sundays and take me out to tea at the Cockpit or Fullers. She was as adorable as ever, but I bitterly regretted that she never came alone. Always there was a different swain in attendance, a young blood in a pinched double-breasted waistcoat – what my father called a gigolo – driving her in a sleek

Hispano-Suiza with several straps round its bonnet, or an elderly sugar-Daddy in a coupé of basket coachwork. My resentment of these swains was not mitigated by the crackling £5 notes which they would slip into my hand on parting. Only rarely did I persuade my cousin to step behind the door of Upper Chapel and let me imprint a chaste kiss upon her tiny rouged cheek.

One result of this novel attachment was a temporary break with the serious Eton set to which I properly belonged, and an alignment with the wrong, raffish set. I now found their brand of cynicism and bravado peculiarly attractive, and their gossip about London night life and scandal the last word in adult sophistication. I passionately wished that I was the son of a divorced Earl with a house in Belgrave Square, a fleet of Rolls Royces with footmen on the box, and a private aeroplane. Cocktails, coquetry and adultery were now the only themes that inspired my leisure hours. To my surprise these new interests were not unobserved by my housemaster who forthwith referred them to my ever vigilant father. He wrote me a furious letter of abuse and warning, attributing my depravity to the bad influence of my cousin, adding that she was no better than she ought to be. I have always remembered these words as a classic example of unconscious hypocrisy.

My father had ceaselessly impressed upon me the indelible disgrace of expulsion from school. No subsequent crime in the long rota of life's circus would have more terrible consequences. Convictions for cheating at cards, theft, rape and murder were doubtless disagreeable records for any public school man subsequently to explain away, but expulsion from Eton would set the seal upon all social intercourse thereafter. Nothing worse could befall him. And here was I with both eyes open to the irredeemable fall from grace deliberately running the risk. To be quite fair to myself I was not absolutely aware of its gravity until too late to retract with honour. It happened like this.

One Friday morning between schools two of my friends from the wrong set, namely David and Roddy, having boasted of recent hair-raising exploits, nodded towards me and said to each other: 'Shall we invite him?' 'To what?' I asked eagerly. 'To join the Dolly Sisters and come to Bray tomorrow afternoon instead of Sebastian who's ill', was the reply. 'It only means cutting six o'clock Absence and bribing someone to answer for you,' they said. 'All you then have to do is walk with us down the Slough road. Nothing easier. You'll find it simply too divine.' Immensely flattered to be considered worthy of taking the place of the dashing Sebastian in some risqué outing, I readily accepted. I knew of course that Bray was strictly out of bounds. But I was wholly unaware what the jaunt would amount to.

At the appointed hour on Saturday afternoon, which was a half-holiday, the three of us met in School Yard and walked off together along the Slough road. When we had got safely beyond Eton and turned a corner we came upon a huge, stationary limousine more glass than wall, of sumptuous carriage work, with a coronet on the door panels and glistening brass head lamps. From the wheel a smiling young chauffeur in green livery and a peaked cap descended. The motor belonged to Roddy's mother who was at this moment in Monte Carlo and presumably unaware of the use to which it was being put. The chauffeur, who was obviously in the know and very acquiescent, quickly opened a door and bundled us inside before we could be seen and reported by a stray master. Once there Roddy pulled down all the pale grey blinds by their tasselled cords. We were safe.

I was amazed to see through the filtered light that the floor of the motor was deeply littered with women's clothes, hats and wigs. From one cardboard box tumbled a torrent of bangles, long amber necklaces, pendants and earrings. In another were pots of cosmetics, powder, lipsticks and rouge. Roddy and David instantly discarded their own clothes and began arraying themselves in long trailing tea-gowns. I was told to do likewise. I was acutely embarrassed but far too feeble to refuse. Fear of disappointing and annoying them was at the time greater than fear of making a fool of myself. The whole nightmarish prospect now dawned upon me. I was, and am, a pitiably bad actor, self-conscious and gauche to a degree scarcely credible. Besides I can honestly say I have never been the least attracted by transvestitism, and the idea of dressing myself up as and playing the part of the opposite sex does not appeal to me. But there seemed absolutely no alternative to making the best of a situation which I foresaw had little chance of success.

Roddy and David however were enjoying themselves no end, and their giggles were accentuated by my embarrassment. The confusion inside the limousine was of course frightful. There was hardly enough room for one, let alone three boys to change, and high though a Daimler model of the mid-1920s was, it certainly did not allow one to stand upright. Consequently by the time we had finished the dresses were rather more crumpled than the real Dolly Sisters would have thought fitting. Mine was probably less creased than the others' because I was obliged to put on a knee-length pleated skirt and silk blouse instead of the tea-gown indicated. My companions having tried the tea-gown on me decided that I was too flat chested to look convincing *en décolletage*. I was much relieved. The female day clothes, however unsuitable, enabled me to wear a cloche hat under which, with poufs of hair from a chestnut wig pulled over my cheeks, I fancied I would not easily be recognizable. Plastered with false jewellery and made up to the eyes, our lashes mascaraed and lips a pillar-box red, the three of us settled down in a stiff row on the back seat. We were now ready and, pulling up the window blinds, let the evening sun fall full on our make-up and the immaculately powdered bosoms of my companions.

I was much dismayed when Roddy directed the chauffeur to drive to Bray by way of Eton High Street. This piece of bravado seemed quite uncalled for. Since I, the least resplendent and as it were the ugly sister of the party, was sitting in the middle I was able by demurely looking down at my feet to be as little conspicuous as possible. But the other two made to my mind a positive exhibition of themselves. While we drove deliberately at a snail's pace through Eton, which happened to be thronged with boys on their way back from the playing fields for lock-up, they did their utmost to draw attention to themselves. David by now was puffing clouds of smoke from a scented cigarette in a long jade holder and smirking to left and right of him. Roddy, looking preposterously haughty, leaned a long, bare arm through the lowered window and trailed with delicately beringed fingers an orange chiffon handkerchief. I did not dare look too closely at the expression on my schoolfellows' faces as they confronted the amazing spectacle of three demi-mondaines shamelessly advertising themselves in the sacred precincts.

When we reached Bray we drew up before a roadhouse, built of half-timber and shiny herring-bone brickwork. I was much impressed by the dignified bearing of my companions who acted as I was once to observe Lady Desborough behave on arrival at a ball at Holland House. Until the chauffeur opened the door of the motor and folded back the rug from their knees they made no effort to move. Then Roddy was the first to make a majestic descent on the chauffeur's arm, followed by David rather more graciously. I sheepishly brought up the rear. Compared with them, who were so sleek and self-assured, I felt like a newly born foal, which my long legs helped me to resemble, lolloping behind two highly bred brood mares. As soon as we were within the roadhouse I recognized the regular screech and thrumming of a foxtrot. Sure enough having crossed the ingle-nooked lounge we came to a hammer-beamed ballroom with walls of punched leather, where a *thé dansant* was just beginning. The room was full of gentlemen curiously dressed in plus-fours, Fair Isle sweaters and dancing pumps, and ladies with Eton crops or shingled hair dyed mahogany or the lacklustre hue of over-ripe corn. Nearly all these ladies wore ankle-length dresses sewn with sequins or beads. Before I had time to consider what I ought to do with myself Roddy and David made a bee-line for the bar, where they ordered themselves a white lady each. Within a matter of seconds they had tossed them down and taken to the dance floor. Dejectedly I watched David being whirled off his feet by an ex-Flying Corps officer with a waxed and pointed moustache. Roddy was already being violently pump-handled by a monocled bounder of unparalleled vulgarity. I was thus left standing first on one leg then on the other, dead sober, deserted, miserable and clearly a wallflower.

The situation was not to be borne. There was only one way of remedying it. Although no drop of alcohol had ever yet passed my infant lips I knew that at last a dire need of Dutch courage was upon me. I too made for the bar and nervously ordered myself a double white lady. The taste was nectar. The effect was instantaneous. Life coursed through my veins; all inhibitions fled. I felt ready for any adventure. It was indeed there for the asking in the shape of – it makes me queasy to recall even after forty years interval – the assistant master who, that half, was teaching me algebra. For, as I turned away from the bar flushed with delicious sensations, I was confronted by – of all people – Mr Hartington-Jones, the mild, respectable, rather po-faced bachelor beak who shared with a spinster sister a house in Weston's Yard. Had it not been for the white lady I should undoubtedly have collapsed in a heap of silk and tulle, and given myself away completely. As it was, I managed to keep my head, which in my unwonted state of euphoria I presumed to be quite unrecognizable beneath the heavy disguise. Mr Hartington-Jones certainly gave no sign of recognition. He merely gave me a long, searching look which I resisted with commendable spirit. Then with a rather nasty leer, which might have meant anything, he asked if I were dancing this one. 'No,' I replied, pursing my lips into a genteel parabolic curve which I imagined became the demimondaine I was meant to be impersonating. I was determined to be as dumb and refined as possible. It is wonderful how easily, after a first stiff drink, one can maintain a silent alibi behind a wig and cloche hat, not to mention an impenetrable mask of make-up. But the moment speech or movement is called for then a degree of acting is imperative. Speechlessness, I thought, might in the circumstances pass for bashfulness – an absurd misconception of a tart's rôle at a roadhouse *thé dansant*, as I immediately realized on seeing David prattling volubly with his partner. But total inaction was not appropriate. When it came to dancing the black bottom with Mr Hartington-Jones my latent resources were strained to the utmost. He was an uninspiring partner, as awkward as I was, and unable, it seemed, to let himself go. Still this ghastly twisting and jiggling was better than sitting out and making conversation, which I feared was bound to betray me – and not only me but the others. At that moment Roddy, anxiously edging towards us in the dance, turned from his partner, and switching off a dazzling society smile, gave me a vicious look like a rapier thrust and hissed in my ear, 'Drop him, you fool!' Soon afterwards the music stopped. Roddy with his back to me gave me a desperately smart kick with his heel as a reminder. I took the hint. With remarkable presence of mind I said with a wry grimace to Mr Hartington-Jones, 'I'm afraid I'm going to be sick,' clapped my hand to my mouth, and bolted to the ladies' lavatory.

For the rest of the evening I waited forlornly in the limousine in the car park. I had not, as I foresaw, been an unqualified success. Yet I was not in absolute disgrace, and my final resourcefulness was even commended. On the way back the three of us speculated whether Mr Hartington-Jones had been at Bray in order to enjoy himself, which seemed unlikely, or was sent by the headmaster as an *agent provocateur*. If that was his rôle then all I could say was – he had not provoked me.

The half drew to a close without further incident. But when I got home for the Easter holidays the portents were bad indeed. My father had already received my school report, which was extremely unfavourable. None of the masters I was up to gave me a good character. I was lazy, surly and uncooperative. I excelled at nothing. In algebra it appeared that I was particularly dense. Furthermore I consorted with some undesirable friends, although no actual mention was made of my having broken bounds and frequented a low grade roadhouse. Either Mr Hartington-Jones had not detected me, or out of uncommon decency had said nothing. Possibly he was reluctant to let the authorities know that he himself patronized so notorious a place. My housemaster recommended that there was little point in my remaining at school beyond the summer half. Eton, he hinted, could do little further for me, and I might just as well make room for some other boy who would benefit from it. My father was naturally in a blazing temper. My mother who could not face up to the recriminations which, she explained, would only make her ill, kissed me fondly goodbye, and sailed away to Canada.

The future was by no means bright. I wondered desperately, now that my most loyal ally had defected, how I was to get through the Easter holidays alone with my father. He barely spoke to me unless to emphasize what a dismal failure I had become, and to what depths of depravity I was bound to sink until I was totally lost from sight in Wormwood Scrubs, Colney Hatch or the Hospital for Incurable Venereal Diseases, he could not predict which. One of the three was bound to claim me until a merciful death and oblivion put a seal upon my miserable and unwanted existence. He gave me at most five years before the process was complete.

A few days later a gleam of sunlight broke upon the depressing prospect. At breakfast, after reading his letters, my father announced in a peculiarly flat voice that Janie Puleston intended to stay one night with us on her way from London to Wales, and would be arriving that afternoon. He added sanctimoniously that, tiresome though it was, he hadn't the heart to say No, because my absent mother would wish us to be charitable to her pathetic, misguided waif of a cousin. 'Of course,' I agreed rather too piously, 'in the circumstances we couldn't very well turn her away.' My father merely gave me a stern look and attacked his second poached egg. Inwardly I was much elated. I was firmly convinced that Janie was coming out of love for me, and I spent the rest of the morning devising how I could make the most of her short and precious visit. Considering how strongly my father disapproved of her he would not, I fancied, want to waste much time on her, unless of course he thought that by doing so he would keep her deleterious influence away from me. Therein lay a possible difficulty. From the moment she arrived it became quite clear that this indeed was my father's motive. He felt bound, against his personal inclination no doubt, to monopolize her. He conducted her round the stables, actually mounted her on his favourite hunter, took her for a ride, gave her a foxhound puppy because she admired it, and at tea time appeared as attentive and charming as my mother could possibly have desired. Janie responded in her most beguiling little-innocent manner. She sat piquantly at the table as though butter would not melt in her mouth, gently teased my father, rolled her great eyes, pouted, and said how much she adored the country and the simple life. Only occasionally did she throw me a patronizing word as though I were seven instead of seventeen. Her tact and circumspection captivated my father, but infuriated me. I was tormented by agonies of acute jealousy, disappointment, and bitterness.

After tea my father asked if she would care to go on the great pond and try out the new punt he had made in his workshop, for he was a splendid carpenter, and excusably proud of his handiwork. There was just time before it got dark. It appeared that nothing in the world made more appeal to little hot-house Janie than being punted in the dusk of a frosty April evening when the chill mists were rising from the water. So off they went with a pile of cushions, rugs and fur-lined coats, while I retired ostensibly to wrestle with my holiday task, which was Sir Edward Creasy's *Fifteen Decisive Battles of the World*. In truth my suspicions were aroused and I was determined to have them allayed, or confirmed. All is fair in love and war, I kept repeating to myself. Quickly I followed the pair at a discreet distance and, while they were launching the punt from the boathouse, ensconced myself like Charles II unobserved in the branches of a huge oak tree overhanging a narrow channel through which they were bound to pass and return. From this vantage point I deliberately set out to spy on them. I clearly overheard Janie's cooing little flatteries – well calculated to seduce a vain middle-aged squire or a romantic teenager – and my father's tender rejoinders. The nauseating dialogue took place as they punted out and back. While the boat was drifting in the open water it ceased. My suspicions were confirmed. I was heartbroken and enraged, and bent upon revenge.

Throughout dinner the two kept up a flow of badinage which I found intensely irritating. I ate in sulky silence. After dinner in the smoking room my father drank port and Janie sipped Cointreau at a card table, playing rummy. I was studiously ignored. Nevertheless I refused to leave them together and sat reading within earshot. In trying to concentrate upon the fate of Miltiades after the Battle of Marathon I was distracted by their whisperings and private jokes, which struck me as extremely juvenile for two people of mature years. At ten o'clock precisely Goddard, the old parlour-maid, came in for last orders. 'And will your ladyship have early morning tea?' she asked Janie, who seemed not to be listening. Whereupon my father rather officiously answered for her, 'No Goddard, she won't.' 'Very good then. Good-night, m'lady! Good-night, sir!' and Goddard ambled off.

I did not fail to detect in my father's remark a premonition which gripped my heart with a chill of despair. However, I continued obstinately to sit with them until bedtime could no longer be postponed. At midnight we all retired upstairs. I piloted Janie to her bedroom, practically pushed her through the door and with a curt goodnight slammed it on her before she had time to say, 'Poor Janie still loves her little cousin velly, velly much,' and offer me a Judas peck on the forehead.

My bedroom was at the end of the north wing of the house which extended practically into the churchyard. By hanging out of my window I could see that of the spare room, where Janie was sleeping, in the west wing at a right angle to mine and just beyond the front stairs. If its curtains were open I could look right into this room. If they were drawn I could faintly discern through them, only when the spare room lights were on, a blurred silhouette of its occupant. Often in the past I had entertained myself with guessing what a visitor was doing by the indistinct movement of his or her shadow, pulling off a shirt, kicking off a shoe, brushing the hair, stretching or even yawning. But I took good care not to leave the light of my room on for fear of being found out like Peeping Tom. Tonight indeed before undressing I hung out of the window till the last moment, that is to say until the spare room lights were finally switched off. My vigil was not long drawn out, for Janie who was no reader in spite of a professed adoration of poetry, having gone through a guest's customary pre-bed antics witnessed by me through the diaphanous curtains, soon prepared for sleep. I too in my abject misery then undressed. But I was taking no chances. I drew the head of my bed close to a spot by the open window where I knew from experience that any light from the spare room, if turned on again, would shine across my pillow. Even upon the heavy eyelids of adolescents hopelessly pining for loved ones a mere twenty yards away sleep must eventually descend. At some time during this night it fell upon mine.

I do not think I slept very soundly. What reason had I to do so? I was in disgrace. My mother was abroad. I was in the custody of my father who openly despised me and whom I openly disliked in return. And now when the cup of love had unexpectedly and tantalizingly been proffered it was dashed from my lips by the one being who gloried in my discomfiture. My father was outrageously flirting with the object of my love and there seemed to be nothing I could do to correct a cruel disorder of affairs. But as I was to discover later in life, an injustice which may appear to be on the point of crushing the soul to smithereens, can be wonderfully parried and changed into swift retribution. Providence gives a mischievous turn to the wheel of fortune and lo! the joker is dealt into the poor rake's hand. And so it happened to me early the following morning soon after dawn, although the shaft of light which suddenly illuminated my pillow did not bring with it immediate comfort. Far from it. I jumped from bed and strained out of the window. Certainly a lamp had been switched on in Janie's bedroom. For a split second I distinctly saw through the drawn curtains two shapes move together. Then as suddenly the lamp went out. There was a stirring among the wood pigeons in the chestnut trees along the drive, and a faint slither of gold reflected from the nave windows of the church.

The worst then had happened. 'The brute, the fiend! the traitress, the bitch!' I exploded with anger against the two of them, grinding my teeth and stamping with bare feet on the fluffy rug beside the bed. My fury aroused that natural courage latent in every human breast and only awaiting the last desperate summons to be released. This morning I needed no white lady with which to face a hideous situation. Not for nothing had I masqueraded as a Dolly sister at Bray. On that occasion I had not acquitted myself gloriously. 'Now', I said slapping my chest, 'we shall see. Even worms turn,' I addressed myself in the looking-glass with an extremely ferocious countenance. No time must be wasted. I must act immediately.

It was I suppose about six o'clock or thereabouts, and the servants were not yet up. In my pyjamas and without slippers I crept out of my room and down the three steps to the landing. To avoid being heard at this hour I would not pass the other bedrooms. So I padded down the creaky front stairs to the ground floor, across the stone flags of the hall, through the baize door of the passage leading to the back regions, and up the back stairs. Like all children I knew intimately every corner, the squeak of every board, the latch of every cupboard of my home. Each room had its peculiar smell, its own light or dark personality, its own strong ethos. I knew as a baby instinctively knows the womb that cradles it how far I dared take liberties with this and that nook and cranny. At the top of the back stairs one had to be careful not to rattle the door with a loose pane opening on to the first floor passage between the front and the servants' quarters. Turning to the left I passed the weighing machines which stood alongside the airing cupboard. Further on, up a step was the housemaids' pantry where the mops, brooms, and pails were kept, and the maids' overalls hung on a row of hooks. Here too for some mysterious reason Goddard kept her morning uniform consisting of a plain blue cotton dress, starched cap and apron. These I hurriedly put on over my pyjamas, tying the apron in a vast bow at the back in the way I had often watched Goddard tie it, and adjusting the cap in a little cracked glass that was propped over the sink. Did my schoolboy face look as swarthy and puckered as hers? Not quite, perhaps, but never mind.

Thus accoutred but still barefooted I retreated post haste down the backstairs. It was essential that I should complete my preparations before the kitchenmaid, usually the first to get up, should make an appearance. Goddard had been expressly told not to call Janie with tea. Consequently no tray had been prepared the previous night. But I knew where the small blue and white tea services were kept in the china pantry, and the silver spoons in the safe. There was, I decided, no need on this occasion actually to make tea, fill the pot, and cut and spread wafer-thin slices of bread and butter. Having laid a token teapot, hot-water jug, cup and saucer, I mounted the stairs once more, carrying my trayload. Having opened and passed through the door with a wobbly pane I paused for a moment in the upstairs passage, and reflected upon the plan of action. My hands were now trembling so violently that I heard the tea spoon rattle sharply against the cup. 'Look here,' I said to myself, 'this won't do. You *must* pull yourself together.' I then forced myself to gloat upon my wrongs and the sweets of a justifiable revenge. This made me feel better. 'And may God give me strength,' I added reverently.

In the way in which I like to imagine that the man who has finally jumped off the top of the Eiffel Tower repines no longer, and before he has reached the bottom even rejoices that at long last a difficult decision has been irrevocably taken, I stepped almost gaily along the upstairs landing. Only for a second did I halt outside Janie's door. Should I, or should I not knock? I knocked, and turning the handle stepped boldly in. Boldly I shut the door behind me. The room was darker than I expected, yet somehow I did not like to turn on the light by the door. It seemed just a bit unsporting to take the enemy totally unawares, in fact rather like shooting a sitting pheasant. Also my innate delicacy prevented me from immediately peering at the bed. However, an abrupt and awkward rustling of bedclothes broke the stillness. Then a muffled, quavering little voice asked nervously, 'Who on earth is it?' Clearing my throat and taking a deep breath, I replied in my best Worcestershire dialect, 'Oim Goddard, m'loidy, with yer taey,' and dumped rather too unceremoniously the tray on the table on that side of the bed whence the voice had issued. 'But I thought . . . ' the voice resumed in a sleepy drawl which did not deceive me, and muttering something about 'too early' died away on a plaintive note. I pretended, just like Goddard whenever it suited her, not to hear for I did not wish to be drawn into conversation more than was necessary. Instead I walked across to the window and viciously tore back the curtains which screeched on their runners, letting in the golden morning light. Having made a loud enough disturbance I then turned round and made a thorough examination of the bed. A few brown curls from Janie's head were just visible on the far side pillow. The nearside pillow had a dent in it but was empty. On the other hand, below it was a huge, amorphous lump under the bedclothes.

I now felt triumphant and fully determined to pursue victory to the bitter end. I went into the bathroom and officiously perhaps – for what young woman of Janie's sort ever had a bath at 6.30 a.m.? – turned on the taps. Leisurely I put down the bath mat and began folding up her stockings and underclothes scattered on the floor the previous evening. The noise of running water gave a wonderful opportunity for the occupants of the bedroom to settle their scores without being heard – and Goddard was just a trifle deaf – provided they were quick about it. This they certainly were. While about my business I could see in the looking-glass over the wash basin what was going on next door. The amorphous lump rapidly disengaged itself from the sheets and slinking from the bed assumed human form. I had a beautiful view of my father's backside straightening itself into a tiptoe run across the room. I remember thinking how comical rather than reprehensible a person looks when caught 'in flagrante delicto'.

So that was that. All had gone according to plan. I remained master of the field. With time to reflect, a variety of emotions rose and fell within me. The first was a nervous relief which almost thrust tears to the surface. But catching in the glass a glimpse of the no less comical picture I made, shame suddenly got the better of

self-pity. I would look and be a fool no longer. Angrily I tore off
Goddard's cap and apron. I did not stop at that. I tore off the top
and then the bottom of my pyjamas as well. Strength and resolu-
tion were best expressed in utter nakedness. Seizing the first thing
that came to hand I bounded into the bedroom; sprang across the
carpet and locked the door into the passage. 'Janie!' I shouted at
her. 'How could you be such a beast? I absolutely detest you!' The
silly auburn curls shook themselves on the pillow, and from a star-
tled, pallid face two enormous eyes peered over the sheets at the
astonishing vision of an avenging spirit in the full sunlight of an
April dawn. Satan and all his host awaiting catastrophic punishment from the Archangel Michael could hardly have been more
surprised than Janie was to see me standing with my back to the
door, barring egress as it were to the gates of heaven, legs wide
apart, and brandishing instead of a shining sword, a long loofah
snatched from the wooden sponge rack. She gave a sharp screech
of alarm like a kitten that has been trodden on, the first natural
sound she had uttered for ages. 'If you do that again,' I shouted
back, now working myself into a passion, 'I will kill you. I really
mean it.' She was apparently about to give vent to a second mew
when I forestalled her. Casting the loofah into the empty grate and
all scruples to the winds, I rushed at her, and like a tornado dived
headlong between the bedclothes.

The reader may ask how, after the lapse of an hour or more, I
contrived to get back to my own room undetected; and furthermore how I managed to avoid what might be termed 'the serious
consequences of my action'. It was perfectly simple. I didn't have to
do either. I walked away as bold as brass, whistling. Neither my
father nor my cousin was in a position to do, far less say anything. I
had got them both in a cleft stick.

IV

THEY

THE SUMMER half of 1926, my last at Eton, passed in a
blaze, not of glory, but of sentiment and song. I was by
orthodox school standards a failure, by Eton ones a 'scug'.
I had excelled in nothing. I had made no mark whatever with the
popular boys or the masters. Unlike the majority of my schoolfellows, I had not yet been fashioned by Eton into a man of the
world. But Eton had done two things for me which I prize inter-
dependently beyond all the gold that glitters. She had provided a
handful of friends to whom I was then more deeply attached than
they ever suspected and to whose memory – since most of them are
dead – I shall be eternally faithful. She had also awakened in me,
through them, a love of literature, the arts and above all civilized
living, from which because of my philistine background, my
comparative poverty and my total lack of creative ability, I was
unable immediately to profit. In other words the friends I made
and the tastes they fostered at Eton were intellectual and aristo-
cratic, whereas my circumstances were low-brow and lower upper-
class. Were I one to set much store by contentment I might decide
that Eton had in the long run done me more harm than good by
raising me above my proper station to a level for which I was not
innately equipped. But I do not. On the contrary I prefer to be in
the running without ever winning – I gloriously lack ambition –
than never to run at all. I am glad that I did not go to a dim public
school, glad that I did not set a ceiling in cricket and football, glad

that I was not churned out a happy philistine with no satisfactions beyond that of being a good fellow.

My memory of that last summer half at Eton is idyllic, and intensely romantic. Examinations were over. I had in the previous December got my school certificate with five credits. There was no longer need for me even to pretend to work hard, and since I was about to leave I certainly did not bother any more with organized games, which I have always considered the most fatuous form of recreation. Instead I revelled in friendship to an extent never approximated since. I look back nostalgically upon those summer months spent either in the School Library discussing books with that dear man, Mr Bendel the librarian, listening to Tom Mitford play Bach in the Music School, reading poetry with Basil Ava and Rupert Hart-Davis, or leisurely sculling in a whiff up the Thames to Queen's Eyot and getting drunk on draught cider with Desmond Parsons in the long grass beside the river under a golden sun which never set. The last week was spent in exchanging photographs with my intimates, and succinctly writing over them To Tom, or Desmond, from Jim, for it was only in our last year that we addressed each other by christian names. What depths of promise, what bonds of affection lay in the discreet superscriptions! I suspect that these few simple pledges meant more to the givers and receivers than those expensively calf-bound and for the most part unreadable tomes perfunctorily distributed by previous generations. I still possess as many as thirty – with titles like 'Inside Sebastopol' (anonymous) and Wharton's 'Wits and Beaux' – given to my grandfather on his leaving Eton in 1863, and all uniformly signed 'from his affectionate friend' – who was probably nothing of the kind – followed by the initialled surname.

The only nagging anxiety throughout this blissful time was what the future held in store for me. Just as the first term at my preparatory school was haunted by fear, not merely of the whole dreadful system but particularly lest the war should last so long that I would be obliged to fight in it, so the happiness of bathing at Parson's Pleasure, or sozzling among the buttercups by Dorney

Lock, was overcast by the prospect of adding up sums on an office stool in Leadenhall Street. The full horror of this fate was actually upon me once I had turned my back on Eton for ever and found myself at home again in Worcestershire, not this time for the holidays with their limited length, but indefinitely unless I quickly bestirred myself.

August and September of this year were miserable months. I was now eighteen and 'no longer a chicken' as my father gleefully pointed out, adding in a menacing tone which I took to be an oblique reference – there was never a direct one – to the lamentable incident of the previous holidays, that I was not responsible for all my actions. Surely I knew what I wanted to do in life? All boys who were good for anything knew long before leaving school whether they wanted to go into the army, navy, Foreign Office (for this career I was far too stupid), Civil Service, or just business. No, I didn't. All these prospects filled me with despair. Secretly I wanted to go to one of the two universities and then spend the rest of my days doing nothing but read poetry on the shores of Lake Como, where incidentally I had never yet been. But my father would not send me to Cambridge, because he had run up debts at Trinity in the nineties, or to Oxford because he was told there were three niggers at Balliol. Besides, apart from being frightfully expensive, universities only gave one worse ideas than those one had already. Although my father was then quite well off he was determined not to give me an allowance, however small, because it would encourage idleness. Never having done a stroke of work himself he was adamant that I must earn my living. He was very certain that 'the revolution', to which the General Strike of that spring had been an ugly pointer, was imminent, and the days of privilege were numbered. 'We must all learn to stand on our own feet now,' was his constant cry. How right indeed he was in both regards if one discounts his certainty of the imminence and the manner of the revolution's coming. For he did not visualize it as merely social and economic. He foresaw it as constitutional and internecine, in fact Bolshevik and bloody. He thought it would break within a matter of months and be accompanied by torrents of bloodshed. He rather looked forward to fighting the enemy to the last ditch from behind the barricades. For this reason he favoured my going into the army, made me practise bayonet charges with a pitchfork at a stuffed sack hung from the branches of the mulberry tree, and himself spent hours polishing his shotguns and stalking rifles, and laying in a vast supply of cartridges and bullets. He made my mother walk about the village with an eighteenth-century sword-stick, of which when the enemy seized the end – a thing he was sure to do – she would be left with the handle of an extremely blunt and rusty blade. Having despatched him with a deft thrust and twist, she must at all costs recover the stick part (which meant loosening the victim's grasp of it, admittedly an awkward task with stiffening corpses) so as to re-sheathe the implement and not let anyone find out how the deed had been perpetrated. If another enemy were to witness it she might not have the chance of repeating the performance.

I was given two months in which to make up my mind what I wanted to do in life. If by 1st October I had not decided, then my father would take whatever action seemed to him fitting. This was fair enough. It was at the same time made unmistakably clear that I was good for nothing. And yet at the back of my mind I believed that somewhere in life there might be a right niche for me, if only I need not be too precipitately thrown into the wrong one. But where? I must confess I did nothing to look for it beyond feebly seeking advice from grown-ups who invariably asked how I wanted to earn my living. To this question I had no answer. Instead I spent hours reading out of sight at the far end of the garden where the water from the great pond flowed into the Badsey brook. The weather this August and September was almost flawless as though in deliberate mockery of my singular depression (these particular months of the year are prone to catastrophe and wretchedness, for example the outbreak of both world wars, not to mention Munich and the Battle of Britain); the weather, I repeat, was almost flawless, just as it was during those bitter months of international crisis. Day after day the sun shone. The garden was suffused with peace and beauty, which made the contrasting conflicts and forebodings within my heart all the more poignant. I shall always associate with my wretchedness those deep, resonant and labial notes of the pond water interminably tumbling down the wide drain, close to the bench on which I sat, endeavouring to immerse the future in the poetry and fiction of the past. The hollow, tragic sound brings back to me that youthful vista of forty, fifty abysmal years (now, alas, all but bridged, although then yawning ahead of me) spent totting up sums from 9 a.m. till 6 p.m. and 1 o'clock on Saturdays, on a high office stool in Leadenhall Street.

Occasional domestic incidents and a visit broke the monotony of this summer desert. One incident nearly got my parents into serious trouble. On a Monday morning some cows broke into the kitchen garden, stampeded and caused a good deal of damage. My father grumbled. My mother shrugged her shoulders and commiserated with Bass, the head gardener. Neither thought much about it. At luncheon while my father was carving the fifth plate of mutton – for by now we three children were suffered to eat in the dining-room – Goddard, standing at the sideboard about to receive it, said casually, 'Oh, sir, I forgot to mention, Mr Bass has taken poison.' 'What?' my father exclaimed, violently splashing a spoonful of gravy against the ancestor whose indifferent portrait was hung over the sideboard on purpose to receive such inundations. 'Yes,' resumed Goddard, ''E mistook it for 'is lemonade.' My father went white to the gills and followed by my mother, rushed to the gardener's bothy. They got there just in time to watch Bass, purple in the face and with the vomit pouring down his chin, expire in an upright chair.

This was a very terrible occasion for my father, because he was indirectly responsible for the tragedy. After the discovery of the cow damage Bass, in the manner of old-fashioned gardeners – a species now practically extinct – had been very upset. Later in the morning he sent word to my father that he needed some prussic acid in order to destroy a wasps' nest. My father who kept such things under lock and key prepared a mixture which he put in a used Kia-Ora bottle and left on a bench in the potting shed. Bass before dying just managed to tell his wife – so she claimed later – that he had mistaken the bottle for the lemonade which she sometimes put for his 'elevenses' on this very bench. He had, he explained, unwittingly taken a long swig of the prussic acid. At the inquest Mrs Bass referred to the fact that my mother (in her unwisdom but intended kindness) had sought to console her with a present of £300. The bereaved widow's words were so phrased that they might well have led to serious consequences for the misguided benefactress. In court both my parents were extremely lucky to get off with a caution not to be so careless another time. The magistrate, being a local squire and an old friend of the family, was aware of their otherwise exemplary characters. My father accepted the discharge as a matter of course, and in recounting the story afterwards would say, 'A friend in need is a friend indeed.' 'But', I reminded him impertinently, 'you always say we ought to stand on our own feet nowadays; and that the age of privilege is over.'

My mother was much hurt by Mrs Bass's seeming ingratitude and hostility. She was also much distressed by the deteriorating relations between my father and me, not to mention those between him and herself. Their marriage during these years was not entirely cordial. Although I am sure she would have done anything, if only she had been capable, to help my predicament, she did not know how to set about it. And since she was satisfied that she could do nothing to improve her own she resolved upon escape by a means which required no explanation, and no embarrassing preparation.

One evening while we were strolling round the garden after dinner arm in arm, she told me that early next morning she was going ballooning. 'Ballooning?' I repeated. I was amazed. 'Yes,' she said, 'I have met the most enchanting friend with a balloon. He is the leading ballooner in England. If he hadn't sprung a leak at the eleventh hour he would have won the Gordon Bennett Race, on his head.' All my mother's geese were swans, and wild ones at that. After I had consented to see her off, I was sworn to secrecy because she did not want to make my dear father anxious. I was accustomed to these subterfuges with which by now I was in full sympathy. She knew this, and she knew that she could trust me.

Next morning we set off together in her little Stellite two-seater for Broadway. 'Back for luncheon?' my father enquired, unsuspectingly. 'Oh, long before,' my mother replied, as she busily opened and shut the throttle. But to me as we chugged off she said, 'I had my fingers crossed.' To her way of reasoning this artifice left her conscience as pure as driven snow and excused the most outrageous untruths. But the fingers had to be crossed before the whopper was uttered, otherwise the absolution did not properly work. While she was waving from the wheel to her friends in the village – and whenever she went out they seemed to be at every cottage gate and window – I noticed how radiantly guiltless and expectant she looked. Indeed I have no doubt she was feeling like a lunar astronaut on the threshold of an epoch-making adventure. She had no luggage apart from her handbag and one heavy object awkwardly wrapped in tissue paper and tied with a blue ribbon.

We motored through Broadway village, and in bottom gear climbed slowly and noisily up the Fish Hill. At the little inn at the top we halted, and my mother asked an old man sitting on a bench with a mug of beer, 'Have you seen a ballooner in these parts?' 'Balloonist,' I ventured to correct her. *No* was the old man's answer, he wouldn't recognize one if he had. But a lorry with a large basket, a pile of dirty washing and some nets had gone down the lane yonder an hour ago. 'That'll be it,' my mother said, and turning the car to the right drove between a pair of stone gate piers towards the Tower, a delightful folly standing on the highest point of the Cotswolds with views, on fine days, over thirteen counties.

Sure enough close to the Tower was the lorry and beside it a man and boy were assembling the balloon. On the grass stood an enormous deep, square basket of the sort out of which Falstaff was tipped into the Thames. Attached to it by a cat's-cradle of ropes and strings an amorphous grey envelope was being inflated from a number of cylinders in the lorry. The clear, crisp morning was disturbed by a gentle hissing of gas accompanied by spasmodic heaves of the netted monster from the ground. 'Here I am, Jack!' my mother called out cheerfully. 'So I see,' was the curt reply, and Jack barely turned a glance in our direction. The ballooner, as my mother would call him, was an odious little man. He had a swarthy, square face, Charlie Chaplin moustache, and a lock of black hair falling over his forehead from a billycock jammed tight upon his crown. He never so much as raised his hat at my mother's approach, an exhibition of bad manners to which I was totally unaccustomed. How or where my mother made his acquaintance I have not the slightest idea. She was invariably a bad chooser of beaux, and this beau – if the creature could claim to be such – was about the worst of her many bad choices I had yet encountered.

But my mother seemed entirely unconcerned by her gruff reception. It was the balloon's glamour rather than the balloonist's which had captivated her. She gaily ran around smoothing out creases in the envelope, adjusting ropes and getting in everyone's way. While the envelope was filling the boy and I were ordered to heave bags of sand into the basket. At last the great swollen dome was raised off the ground, the tubes from the cylinders were detached and the whole apparatus was straining to be off. Indeed it seemed imperative not to delay its flight or thwart it in any respect. My mother was hoisted by the boy on to Jack's shoulders and pitched like a sack of potatoes into the basket. Then the 'ballooner' scrambled after her. The boy was just about to let loose the trail rope when my mother remembered the parcel which she had left in the Stellite.

'I told you not to bring any luggage,' Jack snarled. 'But I must have it, for safety reasons,' she pleaded. I ran to fetch it and undoing the ribbon and tissue paper threw up to her a khaki tin helmet, which was part of her brother's uniform sent home from the front after he had been killed in the war. She immediately clapped it over her shingled head, adjusting the strap under her chin. She had already produced from her bag a pair of outsize goggles which totally concealed the upper part of her face. At a word of command from Jack the boy let go of the rope, the apparatus gave a tug, the basket creaked, and the great dome swung into the air. My mother, in tears of excitement and of sadness at parting from me, was wafted into the blue heavens. I have a clear vision of her blowing kisses with one hand and, in her unflagging determination to be useful, and also to show gratitude to the world for giving her so lovely a treat, vaguely scattering sand and pound notes into the air with the other. I was not to see her again until Christmas.

The boy and I ran around collecting the pound notes, which we divided between us. After getting deliciously tipsy together on Flower's Ale at the Fish Inn we became boon companions before separating for ever.

When I returned alone for luncheon my father was furious. He blamed me for being a party to this disgraceful elopement, which was rather unfair of him. I have never been able to understand why one of an unhappily married couple is always so cross when some unforeseen eventuality removes the other. Instead of showing gratitude my father claimed to be shocked, shamed and injured.

After my mother's flight I felt very wretched. But the pound notes were a wonderful solace. Gritty with sand and redolent of her special scent they were so precious to me that at first it was painful to spend them. But they provided me with temporary independence and a means of defiance. At this time, and indeed ever afterwards, I had no allowance and no regular pocket money beyond what my mother showered upon me at intervals when she remembered. I could not buy a stamp or a cigarette without begging from my father who would dole out with extreme reluctance sixpence at a time, a homily about extravagance and a demand to be shown my account book. For with meticulous precision he himself kept account of every halfpenny spent. For instance, down to the year of his death he would enter in his neat handwriting whenever he went to London, 'Bus ticket Green Park to Down Street, ½d' and 'Evening Standard, 1d.' No item of expenditure was too insignificant to be recorded. What he joyfully imposed upon himself must therefore be mandatory upon his children if they expected to batten on his bounty. The terrible necessity of having to ask for money under these conditions meant that one either refrained until driven by mounting debts to do so, or had to disclose in advance what one wanted the money for. Often enough the reason did not find favour in his eyes, and the sixpence was withheld. Moreover in those unenlightened days it was unthinkable for a boy brought up as I was to take a temporary job of, say, dishing out cups of tea to British workmen at £25 a week or, by impersonating a guardsman in London pubs, hiring out one's body for rather less. Such expedients never once entered our heads. The consequence was that the sons of the well-to-do were often dependent, inexperienced and totally impoverished.

Because of my mother's quixotic fling of money from the balloon I was for the first time in my life able to do something I wanted without seeking parental permission. I telephoned my great friend Tom Mitford, whose home at Swinbrook Manor was thirty miles away, and begged him to take pity and have me stay. The joy of being able to go to Tom's family without having to ask for a sixpence, which I would probably not have received since my father, without knowing Tom, disapproved of him for playing the piano, was unspeakable. Accordingly I tied my suitcase round the handlebars of a discarded motor scooter, which an invalid uncle had given me – I was too seldom able to ride it for lack of sixpences to pay for petrol – and happily set out on my journey.

Readers of Nancy and Jessica Mitford's books have probably concluded that their home life was a sort of nether world ruled by their parents, Lord and Lady Redesdale, in the guise of Hades ('fierce, inexorable and of all the gods the most hated by mortals,' according to Dr Smith's Classical Dictionary, 'whose diet was black sheep and his own children') and his wife Persephone, Queen of the Shades, voraciously raking in souls of the dead and only propitiated by bull's blood. This was by no means my impression. On the contrary, Swinbrook House, where this large and united family then lived, was to me Elysium. Lady Redesdale did perhaps resemble Persephone in her statuesque, melancholy beauty and her capacity to endow her surroundings 'with beautiful views, flowery meadows and limpid streams' (Dr Smith again), for her taste in gardens, houses, decoration, furniture and food was impeccable. She presided, for that is the word, over her beautiful and eccentric brood with unruffled sweetness, amusement and no little bewilderment. Lord Redesdale was admittedly a dual personality. I cannot see that his children had in him much to complain about. Towards them he was Dr Jekyll, indulgent and even docile. Although not a cultivated man he tolerated their intellectual pursuits and allowed them to say and do whatever they liked. He submitted placidly to their ceaseless teasing, particularly Nancy's with its sharp little barb, barely concealed like the hook of an angler's fly beneath a riot of gay feathers. To Tom, whose straightforward nature he understood better, he was touchingly devoted. The devotion was returned and they were like brothers, sharing each other's confidences.

To outsiders, and particularly his children's friends, Lord Redesdale could be Mr Hyde with a vengeance. But then he resented and hated outsiders for daring to intrude upon the family circle. He referred to one of their friends, a shy and diffident boy, as 'that hog Watson' in front of his face, threatened another with a horsewhip for putting his feet on a sofa, and glowered at those who had done nothing wrong with such vehemence that they lost their nerve and usually smashed things, thus provoking a more justifiable expression of his distaste. I was naturally terrified of him, but respected his uncertain temper. I made myself as inconspicuous as possible whenever he was in the room. The golden rule was to keep opinions to oneself in his presence, a difficult rule to observe in this household where the children spent their time arguing and discussing every subject under the sun from religion to sex.

Unfortunately during dinner on the evening of my arrival I unwisely disregarded this rule, with distressing consequences. Lord Redesdale was in a sunny mood, chaffing and being chaffed by the children. Mouselike I ate in silence, smiled when I was spoken to and contributed nothing to the conversation. The cinema was being discussed which led to someone remarking that a film, called *Dawn*, about the shooting of Nurse Cavell was being shown in London. I had actually seen this film and was unduly proud of the fact. Casting discretion to the winds I raised my voice. 'It is an anti-German film,' I said. 'It is high time that we put a stop to anti-German propaganda, now the war has been over for eight years. Instead, we ought to make friends with the Germans.' These or similar words, tendentious but not altogether reprehensible, were what I uttered. The effect was electric. The smile on Lord Redesdale's face was switched off as though by a current. His proud and remarkably handsome features flushed scarlet. The scowl instantly appeared and threw a thunderous shadow across the table. 'You damned young puppy!' he shouted, as he thumped the surface so that the plates and glasses clashed together like cymbals. 'How dare you? You don't know what the bloody Huns are like. They are worse than all the devils in hell. And you sit there, and have the damned impudence –' Lady Redesdale with a pained expression on her dear face put a hand on his arm, and just said in her plaintive, drawly voice, 'David'. He stopped, threw down his napkin, rose from the table and stalked out of the dining room. For a second or two there was a chilling silence, then a chorus of breath let out of girlish lungs. 'Oh gosh!' I said, 'what had I better do now?' The six sisters from Nancy, aged twenty-one, down to Debo, aged six, looked at one another and then chanted in unison:

> 'We don't want to lose you,
> But we think you ought to go.'

Only Tom did not join in this rather callous couplet from the famous jingo music-hall song. He merely nodded assent. 'What? Now?' I gasped, appalled, for it was already half-past nine, pouring with rain, and getting dark. 'We're afraid you simply must,' they said. 'Otherwise Farv really might kill you. And just think of the mess he would make.' There was nothing else to be done. I sloped off into the night.

Worse than the immediate rain was the ignominy of having to

face my father so soon after boasting of the invitation I had received from my friends. When I got out of doors with my small suitcase the rain was indeed something to be reckoned with. Since on my arrival that afternoon the weather was still fine, I had thoughtlessly propped the motor scooter under a tree. Now having been exposed to several hours' deluge it absolutely refused to start. In vain I tickled the carburettor –alas, water had got into the petrol – I unscrewed pieces of pipe and blew down them. I cajoled, I kicked the machine. I ran with it up and down the drive, to no avail. Nothing would make the engine go. There was not a cottage, not a human being within sight. How was I to get help, or get away? It grew darker and darker, later and later. One by one the lights in the house went out. The tinkle of Bach piano fugues ceased. I was drenched to the skin, worn out, cold and desperate. There was no alternative to returning to the house. Somehow I must get hold of Tom and beseech him to take me in for the night unbeknown to his father. So I slunk round to the back. Mercifully a light was still shining from the servants' hall, although it was nearly midnight. Mabel the parlourmaid had not yet gone to bed. I tapped on the window and explained my plight. Surreptitiously she let me in by the back door. While she went to fetch Tom I stood dishevelled and saturated on the linoleum.

To my intense alarm I heard Lord Redesdale's booming voice the other side of the baize door that separated front from back. 'What's this, Mabel? Who is it?' he was shouting. I nearly died of heart failure. The baize door flew open and a light shone upon his god-like face in the doorway. He gasped at the sight of me petrified and dripping like a statue under a fountain. Whereupon he rushed at me with upraised arm. I was more frightened than ever. I expected to be felled like an ox. To my amazement he put his arm round my shoulders, practically embraced me, and said that I was the most splendid boy he had ever known, that my courage and perseverance were exemplary. 'What,' he exclaimed, 'would the bloody Hun not have given for a man of your sterling worth!' I was dragged into his smoking room, a sanctum as remote from his children's guests as the Antipodes, plied with whisky and soda, and told I must stay with him for ever. Eventually I went upstairs to a hot bath and bed in the belief that Lord Redesdale was to be my lifelong friend and mentor. At breakfast next morning he was as cold and distant as ever. But I was allowed to remain at Swinbrook for a week.

The whole of September was spent at home without particular incident. Some two mornings a week we went cub hunting. This meant rising at 5.30 and motoring with my father three miles to the stables of his new lady love and her sister, where he now kept his horses. While the dawn was breaking we would ride to the meet between hedgerows sparkling with silver cobwebs in the slanted sunbeams, and through woods deep in early autumn leaves, still golden, which did not then and do not now spell for me decay, but the rich perennial harvest of past dreams. The brittle beauty of those September mornings was only marred by my absurd scruples. For on our return to the stables my father would stop for breakfast at his friends' house. I out of misplaced loyalty to my mother refused to set foot inside their door. Instead I would, like the prig I was, ostentatiously yet hungrily walk home across the fields in my hunting boots. This behaviour did not help to endear me to my father.

Another occasion that I recall being with him was during one of his expeditions in search of old timbers. He had a passion for black and white houses and mediaeval, or at very latest Jacobean furniture to the rigid exclusion of every other style of architecture and decoration. In these comparatively palmy days he began demolishing his cottages which were of brick, and rebuilding on the site bijou residences of wood and plaster in a mock mediaeval fashion. Over the windows, which were given diamond lattices, thatched roofs were raised like whimsical little eyebrows. Even the adjacent motorhouses were made mediaeval and the hot-water pipes from boiler to cottage (for these residences were supplied with every modern convenience) were dressed with thatch and adorned with straw dollies. Instead of decent rooms with a foot or two of space between one's head and the ceiling the new cottage rooms were so low and studded with rough hewn beams, of which the undersides were a mass of splinters, that no one over five foot six inches – and my father was six foot two – could possibly stand upright in them. These improvements necessitated a great many oak beams, posts and struts. And for some reason which appealed to my father's sense of period the timbers had to be old ones. New timbers were quite out of the question. So he spent days on end motoring round the country persuading farmers to sell him beams from their derelict barns and sheds. He would examine them all with infinite care before selecting those which were truly riddled with death-watch beetle and so unquestionably 'genuine'. The inevitable consequence was that the inhabitants of these 'mediaeval' gems were kept awake at nights by the ceaseless ticking of the worms, and in the daytime had to sweep up handfuls of dust from the rapidly diminishing woodwork.

His capacity for reconciling blatant fakery with the real antique was very remarkable. Although he owned much genuine oak furniture he nevertheless made many replicas with his own hands. I have already mentioned that he was a skilful carpenter. He was also a marvellous joiner and fabricated (not always out of old oak) gate-leg tables, chests and buffets, complete with most convincing bulbous legs and grotesquely carved masks and terminal figures. These objects he buried under a heap of manure in the garden. After six months or so they were disinterred, to be exhibited to admiring friends as vintage specimens.

Any furniture of an age later than oak was utterly taboo with him. Indeed he despised and loathed it. And when he inherited some Georgian pieces he could not be bothered to sell or even give them away as useless lumber. Instead to show his contempt he made a bonfire of them in the backyard.

The last days of September came and went without any mention of the ultimatum of two months ago. I hoped my father might have forgotten. Not a bit if it. The 1st October dawned. At breakfast he appeared, not in his usual country clothes but in what was then considered an old-fashioned lounge suit, of tight drainpipe trousers and coat buttoned up to the chin. All his suits were of the same date and cut, for when he married in 1904 he had ordered a trousseau of twenty-four. Since he kept them immaculately and on no occasion wore the same one two days running they lasted his lifetime. After marriage he never needed to order another. The sight of this particular London suit gave me reason to fear the worst, although precisely what I did not know. The only remark vouchsafed to me while we ate was a slight variation of the familiar refrain: 'The time has now come for you to stand on your own feet.' 'Do you mean to say,' I asked anxiously, 'that I've got to stand on them today?' 'Yes,' he answered.

I was told to pack and be ready to leave at 9.30. Since I did not know whether my ultimate exile was to be in the tropics or the Antarctic a decision what clothes to take would have been difficult, had I possessed the equipment for either destination. As it was, I possessed one decent suit, which had to do for all emergencies. So I put it, plus a clean shirt and twelve volumes of Byron's poetry and prose, into a suitcase. I naturally did not let on about the Byron volumes which I had recently bought second-hand with money given me for my birthday by my grandmother. It happened that my father had already detected them in my bedroom, doubtless with a view to their eventual consignment to the furnace, and was much shocked to find that I had written on the flyleaf of volume 1, 'To Jim from Grannie'. I had done this deliberately in the hope that it might prevent him destroying them while I was staying with the Mitfords. Indeed the precaution worked, although it provoked my father to remonstrate severely that what I had done was immoral. My grandmother had merely given me a £5 note, and to associate her name with the writings of a cad and bounder was not only unjust, but an insult to her.

I knew better than to be even a minute late, and precisely on the stroke of 9.30 we drove away – to London. My father's mania for keeping accounts was only equalled by that for being on time. When about to go on a long journey it was his habit to jot down on paper beforehand all the towns, villages and landmarks on the route, with the exact minute when he ought to pass by them. He kept this list on the dashboard of the motor, and constantly referred to it. Thus the list would begin: 'Leave front door 9.30. Broadway village 9.40. Broadway Tower 9.57. Trooper's Lodge (one with broken chimney) 10.3. Bourton-on-the-Hill Church 10.17. Moreton-in-the-Marsh public lavatories 10.26. Cross Hands Haystack (if still there) 10.39,' and so on, covering several sheets of foolscap. If by some mischance there was a hold-up and we passed Trooper's Lodge at 10.4 instead of 10.3 we would thereafter drive at demonic speed in order not to be late at the Bourton-on-the-Hill church. Contrariwisely, if we were ahead of time – and this was often the case – we would dawdle along, like a crawling bus, in order to reach the next landmark strictly on the schedule. Because my father could not bear to be passed by another motorist, we would drive down the middle of the road, heedless of the frenzied horn-blowing from people on our tail. If – and even in the twenties this did sometimes happen – we had a puncture, all the times on the foolscap pages had to be readjusted, after the wheel was changed and before we could resume our journey.

On this 1st October no untoward adventures befell us. My father drove in stony silence. Only when we reached the London suburbs did he address me. This was to tell me to check the landmarks, which were now so many and at such short intervals that he could not refer to them and keep his eye on the road at the same time. Thus I read out to him breathlessly: 'Hammersmith Broadway 12.11. Plaza Cinema (indecent films) 12.13. Hideous Georgian villa on right 12.14. Swimming Baths on left 12.15,' until we drew up on the dot of 12.45 in front of the Cavalry Club, Piccadilly.

Having washed our hands we proceeded to the dining room, which smelt of stale toast and manly hairwash. We ate frugally in stony silence before moving to the morning room upholstered in black horsehair sofas and armchairs, which smelt of stale cigars and brandy. Here we drank coffee in stony silence. It was only now I was to learn that my poor father had no plans for me at all. Over a second cup of coffee – he must have been desperate, but never showed it – a friend of his, Colonel Battye, came and clapped him on the shoulder. 'Hello, George!' 'Hello, Percy!' 'What on earth are you doing here?' 'I've come to look for a job for my boy. D'you happen to know of one that would suit him? I have to be quick because I'm dining tonight with the Snodgrasses in Broadway – for poker,' he added, looking at his watch which already registered 2 o'clock.

Percy Battye had absolutely no idea of any job, far less one that would suit me, whom he had never set eyes on before and was, I suspected, now assessing with his rapid Cavalry glance to be no chip off the old block. 'Why not try Useful Women in Dover Street?' he suggested with a chortle, and moved on. 'By Jove, what a good idea!' my father said, brightening for the first time that day.

We jumped into the car and drove straight to Dover Street. The useful woman who interviewed us was efficient, but nonplussed. She had few openings for a public schoolboy of eighteen. What had my father in mind? 'Business,' he answered. 'My boy simply must earn his keep. He has got –' he was proceeding, whereupon I took up the worn thread for him by interrupting. 'You see,' I said, 'he has got to learn to stand on his own feet.' For a moment the useful woman seemed confused. As she looked from one of us to the other, she said, 'Er, which of you has to do this thing?' Then grasping the situation, she continued, 'Precisely. May I say how sorry I am for the immediate necessity.' She threw a pitying look at my father's frayed Old Etonian tie. To me she said with a nasty little smile, 'And what sort of business have you in mind?' 'None,' I answered, crestfallen. My father looked very cross, the useful woman looked snubbed. 'My contacts,' she said, 'hardly seem the sort you need. Have you –' and she turned to my father again, 'no business connections with, for instance, the City?' 'None,' my father answered this time, with some emphasis. 'That is why I am here.' 'In that case,' said the useful woman, incredulous and by now rather bored with us, 'I would suggest a course of shorthand and typewriting for your son. I am sure he'll find it won't come amiss.'

My father was delighted and rose to his feet. Murmuring that he must get home in time to change for dinner, he shook the useful woman by the hand and hustled me out into the street. We motored rapidly to Miss Blakeney's Stenography School for Young Ladies in Manresa Road, Chelsea, which had been strongly recommended.

Miss Blakeney was most welcoming. But I was embarrassed by the facts that the autumn term had already begun a fortnight ago, and all the students were girls. As we stood in a bare room heated by a popping gas stove and stuffy with the peppermint smell of twenty pairs of female armpits, I felt depressed and faintly sick. My father on the contrary was beaming on all the heads bowed in concentration over their clicking fingers. Without putting to Miss Blakeney any questions for fear, I suppose, lest she might raise objections and not take me, he whipped out a cheque book and there and then paid her for a twelve months' course in advance. 'At the end of this course he will be fully equipped for any sort of directorship?' he then enquired. 'Well, er, I daresay,' said Miss Blakeney without much conviction. 'And if he isn't,' my father resumed, 'it will be entirely his own fault, won't it?' 'Well, one might say so,' said Miss Blakeney. 'Excellent!' he concluded, beaming again upon the girls who, when I got to know them later, used to say what a jolly old toff he must be.

My father, pleased with this fairly satisfactory outcome, looked at his watch again and remarked that he really must be going back to Worcestershire. We left Miss Blakeney's door together. My father got into the motor and, starting the engine, addressed me standing on the pavement. 'Whatever happens,' he said, 'you must work hard. Luckily those girls don't look too attractive. Oh! I nearly went off with your luggage.' He really was quite jolly as he handed me the suitcase. At last he seemed to be getting rid of me. 'Good bye, old boy!' I was dumbfounded, and only just had the courage and sense to say, 'But, Papa, where am I going to live?'

'Oh, damn it all!' my father exclaimed. 'I hadn't thought of that. We'll have to go back to the Useful Women. It really is maddening. I'll be frightfully late for the Snodgrasses.' I felt horribly guilty.

A perceptible shadow flickered across the useful woman's face as we walked once more into her office. 'And what can we do for you this time?' she asked. I have frequently noticed that when an individual in addressing another individual uses the first person plural he, or she, is denoting either solicitude ('We are feeling a trifle poorly today, are we?') or boredom ('We are not amused'). The second sentiment was clearly induced by our case.

'I want somewhere respectable for my boy to live,' said my father. 'Nothing too expensive, eh!' 'Naturally,' was the answer. The tone of voice in which this adverb was enunciated nettled my father. 'Well, not absolutely dirt cheap,' he went on. 'Say full board at thirty shillings a week.' After a good deal of telephoning and some not very forcible bargaining by the useful woman, we were given an address on a sheet of paper. My father stuffed it into his pocket without properly looking at it. 'It is in South Kensington,' he said. 'It is,' said the useful woman. 'And if you come back again I may be out, having a cup of tea. So, good afternoon!'

When we got near South Kensington station my father took out a piece of paper from his pocket and glanced at the address. It was quite unknown to him. We had to ask the way from several passers-by. We were eventually directed to a down-at-heel back street; and we stopped before a door, over which a naked electric bulb emitted a dull red glow through the fanlight. I was plunged into gloom at the prospect of lodging in this cheerless quarter.

'You wait in the motor,' my father said, 'while I just go and settle things.' He briskly trotted up the steps and pulled at an insecure bell handle. A raucous clanking responded from the basement. Immediately a cluster of female heads peeped through dingy lace window curtains. After a second pull a young lady, not entirely ill-favoured, with an olive complexion, raven hair and flashing teeth, suspiciously opened the door which she held ajar with one foot. 'Che vuole, carissimo?' she asked. 'What did you say, my good woman?' my father replied coolly. All she did was to giggle. My father, usually so polite, turned his back on her and without further ado walked down the steps. As he slammed the car door behind him he said to me, 'It won't do. Niggers.' Then fumbling again in his pocket, 'Curious thing,' he said, 'I could have sworn the

80

damned Dover Street woman gave me that piece of paper.' I wondered, could the useful woman, who clearly did not take to us, have
written down this address in deliberate malice. It seemed improb-
able. Or had Colonel Battye slipped it into my father's pocket as a
sort of Cavalry Club joke? The moment was not propitious to
investigate either alternative with my father. Anyway, after further
fumbling, another paper, with another address, emerged from the
same pocket.

Our next stop was No. 14 Onslow Gardens. This time my father
sent me to the door, perhaps fortunately, because it was opened by
a motherly old lady who was the proprietor of the establishment.
She had very short legs and a plump body like a hen's. Like that
domestic bird she was also both cosy and sharp. I liked Mrs
Roxburgh at once. On the doorstep I explained to her my require-
ments and my father's circumstances. 'He's broke to the world,' I
said. She smiled kindly, and yet incredulously. 'Of course I'd like to
take you, dear. But do you mean that thirty shillings a week is the
most your father can afford to pay, a man with a car like that?' she
said, pointing to the sleek Minerva. She had not yet spotted the
frayed tie. 'I'll deal with him,' she added, with a wink. Stumping
down one step she beckoned him into the house.

I need hardly say that Mrs Roxburgh was successful. She asked
for £2.10.0 a week, and got it, in advance by cheque, just as Miss
Blakeney had. My father was not a little put out because he was
unaccustomed to people, least of all women, bargaining with him.
In justice to his standards of conduct towards women I believe he
would, albeit with extreme reluctance, have paid Mrs Roxburgh
£210 a week, had she asked for it, rather than haggle with her. He
only haggled with his family.

The whole transaction was concluded within five minutes of our
arrival. During this time my father visibly itched to be heading for
the Snodgrasses. 'I expect she's better than she looks,' he whispered to me encouragingly, as soon as he could decently slip away,
'although she's a bit of a money grubber. However, I'm sure you'll
be happy here.' I was – up to a point.

V

THEO

BEYOND THAT point lay vague, immeasurable longings. What they were exactly it took me years to formulate. Mrs Roxburgh was kind. She made no positive demands upon my spare time which was considerable, because my hours of work were only from 9.30 to 5.30 and 1 o'clock on Saturdays. Until the last war all offices were open until luncheon time on Saturday, the morning of that day never being part of the weekend as it normally, and I am sure rightly, is now. The nature of my work was such that I could hardly be expected to carry on with it after hours. There is a limit to the amount of shorthand and typewriting a person can do daily. Mrs Roxburgh, I repeat, did not expect me to wait upon her or accompany her on expeditions in the evenings or at weekends. Indeed I do not believe she ever set foot outside her house, nor did anyone apart from ourselves set foot inside it. By ourselves I include her gentle daughter, who was rather pretty in a hang-dog way, with a quiveringly sensitive and lachrymose chin. She was about twenty-five, married, but with no visible husband. She possessed a snapshot of him – he looked about sixteen – the only evidence of his existence. He had for some unspecified reason already deserted her.

There was also a strange, middle-aged figure, known to us as the Bean, who led a troglodyte existence in the basement, and wore bedroom slippers from morning till night. He cooked and did all the housework and shopping. Mrs Roxburgh spoke of him in a pitying manner, letting it be supposed that the Bean had known better days, but was now penniless and living upon her charity. In return for free lodging and board the poor Bean in a quiet way must have earned his meagre charity many times over. I never once heard him complain, or indeed speak, but his sighs were terrible. They were long and regular and made the basement shake worse than the Underground. He was rather handsome, also in a hang-dog way, and his chin was no less quivering and lachrymose than Mrs Roxburgh's daughter's. Altogether the household of 14 Onslow Gardens was rather mysterious, and yet eminently respect-able. I always felt something needed explaining. But it never was explained.

Undemanding though Mrs Roxburgh was, she simply loved gossip. I was not averse to listening to it, although I had precious little to contribute. It was amazing to me how someone so appar-ently cut off from the great world as my landlady, knew so much about it. There was no titled woman with whom she was not on the most familiar terms, and to whom she did not refer by her christian name, and if she had one, her nickname. Thus Lady Ilchester, who if Burke's Peerage may be relied upon was baptized Helen, became on Mrs Roxburgh's lips Birdie, and Lady Shaftesbury's prosaic Constance turned to Cuckoo. I would learn how Birdie was com-plaining only the other day to Ethel (Mrs Roxburgh, who was above a nickname) how Cuckoo's pin money was five times more than hers, just because Shaftesbury's earldom was of older crea-tion, which seemed a shame. 'And what, Mrs Roxburgh, did you say to Lady Ilchester?' I asked. 'I advised her,' came the considered answer, 'to dispute the date of Cuckoo's husband's creation.' Then, 'I never did think much of that Fruity,' Mrs Roxburgh resumed, jumping rapidly like the bright little hen she was from perch to perch. 'And I was only saying yesterday to Louey Liverpool that he'll bring the monarchy down, sure as eggs are eggs – not that you can be sure they are anything of the sort these days – if David will be seen driving to night clubs with Fruity, and if you please, in one of May's Daimlers! Baba's all right of course. Still, perhaps

Fruity's less dangerous than Ramsay. And have you seen Lossiemouth, my dear? I couldn't even find the place. I doubt it if actually is a *place*. Circe Londonderry must be mad.'

At eighteen I was duly impressed, but quickly became bored with this particular topic. It was not Mrs Roxburgh's only one, although her favourite. She had another which interested me rather more. It was a bit of a struggle to get her off the social, and on to the literary plane. Yet her acquaintance with men of letters was fairly wide, though possibly not so close. After all, writers and artists mattered less since their private lives did not feature so often in the pages of the *Tatler*. Nevertheless they mattered. I soon learnt that to attempt an abrupt change of the conversation had no success whatever. The break had to be brought about gradually and with cunning. I would introduce the name of someone who had a foot in both the social and literary camps, like this. 'But surely, Mrs Roxburgh, isn't that particular corner of the Scotch Tea House in which Birdie was complaining to you the other day about Cuckoo the very one where, you once told me, Bogey Harris used to take Mrs Humphry Ward?' This was drawing a bow at a venture.

'Dear old Bogey! Dear Augusta!' Mrs Roxburgh would waver for an instant, then fall headlong into the trap. 'I haven't seen her for some time now.' This was not surprising since she had died in 1920. 'A remarkable woman. If it weren't for that Tasmanian accent her novels would have far larger sales. The best of course is *Lady Rose's Daughter*. I knew her uncle Matthew Arnold. Such a pity he died catching a bus. Not quite quite really. Sir Edmund always says it's fatal to run after buses and women. Which reminds me, Gosse and T. J. Wise. "Don't trust that man, Sir Edmund," I said, "further than you can spit. Remember William Henry Ireland and *Vortigern*." Mundy was most grateful to me for the warning.'

The odd thing was that Mrs Roxburgh was by no means a fool. She read voraciously, and she certainly pored over Burke's Peerage and Landed Gentry, as well as Eve's Diary and Lord Donegall's gossip column. She lived in a world of perfectly harmless make-believe. She wove around the nobility and the eminent a haze of romantic moonshine in which she reigned supreme. Through this haze she picked her way towards her victims with remarkable agility, seldom putting a foot absolutely wrong, and not always absolutely right. Although she knew none of the élite she nevertheless made them speak and behave in a manner not so entirely uncharacteristic that a simple-minded listener was not often deceived. Yet in spite of her ceaseless chatter about other people's doings, she never vouchsafed a word about her own origin or past. It was quite clear that her origin had been a sad and her past a difficult one.

Since Mrs Roxburgh inhabited the small ground floor room leading off the passage, or hall, by the front door, it was sometimes awkward to elude her when one was not in the mood for reminiscence. But I must admit that I spent several diverting hours of my first London winter in her company. After the polished furniture, bright chintzes, bowls of flowers and overt cheerfulness of my home in the country, 14 Onslow Gardens was dingy and subfusc. Thickly meshed, greying cotton curtains helped to obscure the grimy plate glass windows. The furniture was uniformly black, one piece being indistinguishable from another. Sofa and chairs were upholstered in beige plush, sticky to the touch. But when at half-past four on a Saturday afternoon the pavement lamp outside curdled the yellowing fog, and the Bean, without apparent summons, shuffled into the room to dump a dish of crumpets and a brown teapot in front of the gas fire, the atmosphere became cosy. Mrs Roxburgh sat fluffed up on the edge of a tall 'art nouveau' chair, her little legs barely reaching the rung several inches above the carpet. With her left hand she held high a dainty cup and saucer, the little finger perceptibly crooked. With her right she kept adjusting a voluminous brown hat which totally hid every feature of her face except a twisted, wicked little mouth. I never saw her morning, noon or night without that hat which concealed so much mischief, and from under which ebbed a continuous burble of merriment and warm-heartedness.

If Mrs Roxburgh afforded me a peep into a world of fantasy –

and with shame I recall how occasionally I would quote as authoritative her less sensible statements, such as the assurance Swinburne gave her that Watts-Dunton had in youth been a female trapeze artist – Rupert Hart-Davis was a link with a world peopled with substantial figures. He too had recently left Eton, but had lost no time in deciding what he wanted, which was to go on the stage. I think he soon discovered that this was not his true vocation. But so long as the enthusiasm lasted he worked extremely hard at a drama school. When he had a free evening he often invited me to his flat, then at the top of his father's house in Hans Place. His large living room made a tremendous impression upon me. It was the most civilized room I had ever entered. The walls were lined from floor to ceiling with books that had been read, the spines of their immaculate jackets flickering in the golden light of a deep coal fire. The air of well being and culture was something beyond my wildest dreams of attainment. For Rupert's kindness to me during that winter I shall always be grateful. He was then purposeful, busy and contented. Yet he spared time to discuss poetry and lend me books. His enthusiasms made it impossible for me to be self-pitying in his company, which was wholly to the good. In those days he looked like a big Airedale puppy, affectionate, boisterous and intensely extrovert. Within a very short time he got married.

He was the only friend I saw in London, at intervals. Grinding poverty prevented me getting in touch with any of my other Eton friends. In fact I deliberately avoided them, and hoped never to run into them in the streets. I suffered from false pride, believing in that desperately puritanical way that one should not accept hospitality unless one could return it. And I could repay nothing in terms of money. My total expenditure a day was one shilling, or at most 1/6d – the cost of a midday snack at the counter of a tobacconist-cum-café in the King's Road. For the shilling I could get tomato soup and cottage pie, which was filling, and so long as butter was not included, any amount of white bread free. Whenever I could afford the extra sixpence I would order ginger pudding with a taste like the smell of Rentokil, and a glutinous white sauce, like stickfast in substance and tastelessness. Mrs Roxburgh's pension terms were inclusive of breakfast and dinner. On weekdays Miss Blakeney's establishment provided tea and a biscuit. I seldom went hungry although for months on end I spent not a halfpenny over and above my strict budget. I naturally walked to the Stenography School in Manresa Road, and so never had occasion to spend money on a bus or the Underground. Sometimes the toe or sole of my shoes would come off. During these crises I was as near to standing literally on my own feet as my father could have desired. I tied the leather on again with string until one of my mother's fitful pound notes arrived, when I had the shoes properly repaired. Books, if not lent me by Rupert, could be got from the public library. I never went to the theatre (unless Rupert managed to get me a free ticket) or a cinema. In some reprehensible way I got a kick out of managing not to spend. The utter penury of those days has, I much fear, made me rather mean, at least pennywise, so that I still suffer pangs of guilt every time I take a taxi or spend money on myself which is not absolutely necessary.

My circumstances made it quite impossible to take out girls, or even to get to know any, with the exception of the girls at the School. And by them, as my father foresaw, I was not attracted. They were a peculiarly brash and uninviting lot. Besides, my being the only male among so many made me shy and on my guard. The fact that they had been working at the course longer, and were naturally quicker and defter at shorthand and typing was, to say the least, humiliating. I have since learnt what I did not then suspect, that the best typists (not secretaries) are made from the uneducated, who allow their fingers to react without the obstruction of thought. One fairly plain girl, Gertie, was particularly nice to me. She was an unboastful, ductile creature, highly proficient at shorthand, reaching some unprecedented speed long before the course was finished. She tried to impart to me the secret of her proficiency out of the sheer goodness of her heart. I got to know her family well. They were sweet working-class people who lived in a small Regency house, approached by steep steps in Trafalgar Square (later razed to the ground, rebuilt with neo-Georgian houses for the rich, and re-named Chelsea Square). To my surprise her parents also were wonderfully kind and pressing with invitations to high tea, which I always declined out of motives of false pride. The young seldom realize that people are only too ready to be nice to them just because they are young. Perhaps this is as well, otherwise they would surely trade on it. Furthermore, the better looking the young, the kinder the old of both sexes are to them. And I was not in those days positively hideous. Sometimes people, and not only the old, are too kind to the young. Gertie certainly was too kind to me. She was also suppliant in a speechless sort of way, which I found eventually irritating.

It was no good. She had absolutely no glamour for me. The episode with my cousin Janie was still recent and the little scar had not completely healed. Besides, rat poor and ineligible though I was, I could no more have had an affair of the heart (as opposed to the senses) with a member of the lower classes than bicycle on a rope across the Niagara Falls. This is not a fact of which I am either proud, or ashamed; but it has to be faced. It cannot be explained by my background which was not exalted. I was brought up among simple country people, and carefully taught by my parents to treat everyone alike. The consequence is that I do not discriminate in day-to-day relations with people. I never feel superior to anyone, nor the least awkward among people who may belong to a lower (or indeed higher) social grade than my own. On the other hand the middle and lower classes (I refer to the Anglo-Saxon, not Latin) are horribly self-conscious when out of their own environment. Since I do not care to stay in their environment for long and they are ill at ease in mine, there is no mutual territory on which heart-felt intimacy between us can very well take place.

I am acutely conscious of and amused by class distinctions. I love them and hope they endure for ever. They are part of the spice of life, as is shown by the fact that they have always been a chief ingredient of the world's greatest fiction. To claim that they do not or should not exist is as hypocritical and silly as to pretend there is no difference between white and black men. Human relations would be duller without them. Class barriers are a different matter which no sensible person would advocate. They are in any case rapidly being pushed down.

I feel deeply humble in the presence of manual workers because of their skill, which I am totally without, and their physical courage, which is its usual accompaniment. But I cannot be intimate with them, and I consider it cant to pretend what one does not feel. I do not on this account consider myself any more snobbish than the robin which is incapable of mating with the sparrow. Janie, with whom I was besotted for several months, had it is true the brain of a sparrow, but not the dun plumage. She was totally uneducated. Yet she and I stood on some common ground, with which our consanguinity had nothing to do. We shared some indefinable herd instinct. Was our bond language? A sense of the ludicrous? Certain basic values, true or false? Was it simply a hereditary gentility, that misunderstood and disparaged quality which I believe nevertheless to have a valid efficacy?

Poor Gertie's lack of glamour was not mitigated by the drabness and ugliness of her parents' house, which surpassed that of Mrs Roxburgh's. However we continued to lunch together, although she, unlike me, could afford pudding every day, and would even offer to pay for mine. This I did not allow. I suspect that with her quick intuition she guessed how poor, and certainly how absurdly proud I was, because she soon ceased to press the point. Often she pretended she did not want pudding either, when I was sure she did. In the school our liaison became a recognized fact, and when in such circles young people are looked upon as plighted, no one else bothers to speak to them again. The arrangement therefore had its advantages, and for the rest of the stenography course I saw no reason for disillusionment. In any event it would have been hard to bring about without causing heart-searching and distress. And I was never deliberately cruel. When the course was over and Miss Blakeney's establishment behind me the break with Gertie was automatic. By a curious coincidence I was able years later to benefit her family. In the next war by absolute chance I discovered my soldier servant to be her younger brother. He was a jolly, picaresque character. While I was away in hospital he stole my gold cigarette case and links. I hope they served as some indirect recompense for any disappointment I may have caused his sister.

Incompatibility of demeanour and deficiency of mutual interest called a halt to relations with Gertie before they had properly progressed. Meanwhile the search for a soul mate, only lately launched, gathered momentum. I was naïve enough not to realize that this search usually lasts a lifetime and is a vain one. But my extreme loneliness in those days prompted a belief that the quarry must be round the next corner, waiting to be transfixed. One of life's great mysteries seems to me the nobility of the young, considering man's certain inheritance of original sin, in the Thomist sense, by which I do not mean sin narrowly identifiable with concupiscence – on this subject I have something to say immediately – but with absence of general righteousness. How is it, I ask myself, that callow, untamed youth, so newly endowed with the old Adam's ruthless propensities, often cherishes and fulfils the highest ideals and has the will and power to sublimate physical desires? With jaded middle age, which ought at least to be temperate, the appetite grows as the capacity to digest decreases. With lusty youth, potent and practised, the sexual act often becomes in love-making wholly secondary. At the age of eighteen I gave sex little thought. It presented no terrors and no intrinsic importance either. It was certainly not a thing to be pursued for its own sake. The idea of sex without love rather shocked me, whereas love without sex could be quite welcome, and by love I mean not just affection, but passion. I was no doubt intensely romantic and silly. But silly or not, I truly believe I was then nearer nobility of soul than I am now, in spite of the subsequent years' accumulation of a little understanding.

Thenceforward I was repeatedly falling in love with someone or other, and it did not seem to me to matter whether with woman or man, provided the one was womanly and the other manly. In other words whichever sex happened to be the object of my passion, that passion was in my eyes perfectly normal and praiseworthy. (Perversion, on the contrary, strikes me as being a delight in the transmutation of natural qualities, a thing which I have nothing against in principle but which does not suit my metabolism.) Furthermore I could be genuinely and deeply in love with more than one person at a time, a state of affairs with which most people have little sympathy, particularly the contemporaneous loved ones. They are inclined to be disapproving and censorious. But here again, I do not see why a person has to be blamed, or reviled, for indulging in multiple sentiments if these come quite naturally to him and are harmless to the world at large. I have never been in love with more than three people at once, and then not for longer than six months. They were a very exacting, but wonderfully exciting six months in which I experienced an almost mystical fulfilment. I reached heights of ecstasy wherein I came closer to God than ever before or since. The experience taught me for the first time the meaning of the Trinity of the godhead, the virtues of whose Persons by some divine dispensation I was able to identify with the peculiar character of my three loved ones. After all a man's reserves of love, both human and spiritual, are, unlike money, inexhaustible, and do not have to be rationed among the recipients.

Without perhaps realizing it I was during my winter in London vulnerable. Anybody happening to cross my solitary path might have turned my head, so long as there was a measure of cerebral affinity between us. As I must already have indicated, I was never invited to parties. I did not think this a deprivation because I hated the idea of them, and when later I was invited to some I hated being at them. But my attitude was a mistake. The Twenties were the last carefree social decade which western civilization has thoroughly enjoyed. For the bright young people with money they must have been unalloyed fun. No visibly menacing clouds from the continent darkened the sky. Communism was still an isolated threat and the remote impact of its initial horrors had not yet been intensified. Fascism and Nazism were still to be experienced. The harrowing Thirties were not even on the horizon. The high rate of unemployment at home was certainly deplorable, but was regarded by the compassionate as an evil that must shortly be overcome, as it eventually was. In those days I never gave politics or world affairs a thought. I did not even glance at Mrs Roxburgh's *Daily Sketch*. The most I did was to cast an eye over the pages of her thumbed and out-of-date *Tatlers*. I was solely concerned with my own day-to-day problems, as I imagine 75 per cent of the British population still are. Since the ordinary citizen is powerless to alter or ameliorate events, how sensible he is to remain a complacent ostrich. He need merely rouse himself to think and vote once every five years.

Dinner in Onslow Gardens was over by a quarter to eight at latest. The long evening would then loom ahead. Often I did not want to settle down and read, and going to bed was out of the question. So pretending to Mrs Roxburgh that I was calling on friends (practically non-existent) I would walk round London for hours, sometimes until I or the soles of my shoes were completely worn out. These repeated excursions passed without incident. I was far too shy to speak to a soul. I never entered a pub because I had no money and because I had never known my father and his friends to do such a thing. I wandered in and out of mews, down narrow alleys, along the river and round the several parks without once having a disagreeable encounter. The London I got to know was as safe after dark as our village street in Worcestershire in the daytime. Also it was still a beautiful city, a thing now hard to credit.

On a February evening at half-past eight I found myself in Covent Garden outside the Opera House. The day had been one of those precociously mild, clear days of earliest spring. Even in Onslow Gardens one could see the fresh earth heaving and hear the crackle of crocuses opening. There was in the air that infinitely disturbing whisper as from distant Siren voices inviting one to take wing, fly anywhere and make a fool of oneself. Far from stuffing one's ears with wax and tying one's body to the mast, one longed for the sea nymphs to board the ship. There is no time of year when one can feel more restless and miserable. Usually the voices are less audible after nightfall when the curtains of winter descend again.

Nevertheless standing outside the entrance of the Opera House, titillated by that delicious smell of fruit and exotic flowers from the market, and watching the rich get down from their limousines, the women wrapped in chinchillas and sparkling with tiaras, the men in sombre black tails and cloaks and carrying opera hats and white kid gloves, I felt more than usually dissatisfied with my lot.

While the flood of pampered humanity was swirling through the *porte-cochère* I fondled in my pocket a £1 note which had floated on to the breakfast table that morning from an envelope addressed in my mother's handwriting. No letter had accompanied it but four old laundry bills which had evidently got there by mistake. On the blank parts of the solitary £1 note were scribbled in ink the words, 'Do hope darling you remember to brush your teeth, Mummie.' This favourite trick of my mother's embarrassed me for I always feared lest a shop might refuse to accept the King's currency thus disfigured. Suddenly, a vernal impulse seized me. For once let a few extra ginger puddings go to hell! And let my only spare pair of shoes, which were awaiting ransom from the cobbler, be damned! I too would go to the opera.

For half a crown I bought a ticket for standing room in the gallery. I had never been inside an opera house before. While I ran up an interminable staircase in the wake of other late arrivals expectancy mounted to fever pitch. I heard the orchestra cease tuning. At the top a crepuscular light disclosed a precipitous ter-raced cliff, the edge of which I had just reached. Only a rail seemed to protect the standers from rolling down the cliff and into the yawning chasm far below. Immediately all the lights in the stalls and boxes were lowered and extinguished. The conductor waved his baton, the orchestra struck up the overture, and the curtain lifted, to reveal Leporello in the first act of *Don Giovanni*.

I will not elaborate upon this classical performance under Bruno Walter, in which the stars Frida Leider, Lotte Lehmann, Elisabeth Schumann and Mariano Stabile took part. To my untutored ear their singing was faultless. I was ravished by the sound and specta-cle. The whole production moreover became a magical background to an irrelevant experience. Beyond the first moment of excitement I can now only distinctly remember Theo. Can I ever forget him? He was the most sympathetic person I have met in a longish life. This is, of course, an inadequate thing to say about someone whose character and beauty I quickly judged to be seraphic. Theo must have been standing in the gallery before I appeared beside him. I suppose he first noticed me looking slightly dazed after my hurtle from the London streets into this world of enchantment. Before I could take in what was happening on the stage he handed me his programme, and with a cigarette lighter enabled me to glance quickly through it. The gesture was spontaneous and characteristic of everything he said and did thereafter. Immediately and unaccountably we were friends before a word had passed between us. In the glow from his cupped hands I caught a glimpse of a Renaissance profile like one of those candlelight portraits in chiaroscuro by Bronzino. He was, as he told me later, exactly my age, and had only just left his public school.

An experience of supreme happiness is difficult to communicate, and its outward manifestations must be banal to a third person. In the first interval we walked round the market; in the second we had a drink at the bar. When the performance was over we walked away together as a matter of course, and had supper at the Café Royal. We sat upstairs over Hamburger sausages and lager, which exhausted the remainder of my mother's pound as well as his contribution. What do rather earnest boys of eighteen talk about? I retain no accurate record of our conversation, but I know he explained how Mozart, of whom I had known next to nothing before this evening, was the purest artist who ever lived. When I complained of not understanding certain passages of the music, he said 'But didn't you enjoy them?' He was the first person to teach me that the purpose of art, and knowledge, was to give pleasure. Until that moment I was totally unaware of this homely truth. On the contrary I had thought of art as a deadly serious matter like algebra, but for some reason best known to myself more uplifting; and a desirable thing to be approached and taken with respect and awe like the Sacrament. To equate it with enjoyment was daring and revolutionary. I felt that a weight had been lifted from my intelligence.

Later we discussed in the manner of adolescents the relation of art to life, the meaning of existence and the pursuit of ideals. Having disposed of these cosmic problems we discussed ourselves without one shred of reservation. It was like peeling two artichokes. Off came the hard, outer, protective leaves in a hurry; then the soft, inner tendrils with caution. The stark centres were exposed, succulent and ready to be devoured. It is a horribly trite thing to say, but we truly laid bare our souls. When it was time to leave I knew him and liked him better than any human being in the world.

Since he had to go north of Regent's Park to his parents' house and my direction lay westward, we parted on the steps of the Café Royal. 'When shall we meet again, Theo?' I asked, for we were on christian name terms already. He was to accompany his parents into the country the following morning. So he replied: 'The very day I get back. I will telephone. In which case we had better take each other's surname and address.' He grinned. I grinned too for it did seem strange for two people to be so united, yet each to be unaware who the other was, and where he lived – a peculiar circumstance which was to recur later in my life. I tore a page out of my pocket book, halved it, and handed him one piece of the paper. He wrote his name, address and telephone number on it propped against the glazed door of the restaurant. He lent me his pencil, one of those cheap silver screw pencils with a cap and short india rubber on the end, with which I wrote on my half of the paper. It was rather dark on the pavement where we exchanged, as we supposed, our papers, and lingeringly clasped hands. 'It won't be longer than four days at the very most, I promise faithfully,' he said. 'Good! And here's your pencil,' I said, handing it back to him. 'No. Keep it. After all, what's mine is yours now,' was his reply. 'Righto! Then you must have this,' I said, offering him my old gunmetal Ingersoll watch, which was practically valueless, but all I had. 'But you'll need it?' Theo asked. 'No, I won't; not till we meet again.' He took it. 'I'll love to have it – till we meet again then,' he repeated, adding, 'Next week, for sure,' and was off. For a second or two I watched him walk up Regent Street. Once he turned his head and smiled. Then I crossed the street, and striking up Piccadilly, walked all the way back to South Kensington.

I was in that seventh heaven in which, according to Mahomet, a man has 70,000 mouths, each with 70,000 tongues which in 70,000 languages chant the praises of the Most High. My gratitude found expression in soundless song. Here was someone who had come out of the blue to alter the whole course of my existence. I would conceivably be able to enrich his. What would we not mean to each other? What did we not mean already? I had long envied twin brothers who shared one mind, and in all other respects double capacities. And now I had found an even better substitute in someone whose greater intellect I respected. He too, thank goodness, was poor. In my pocket I tightly clutched, no longer my mother's crisp pound note but the precious bit of paper, the key to this new friendship.

It was long after midnight when I slipped through the door of No. 14 and crept upstairs to my room. I put the folded paper on the side-table, threw off my clothes and jumped into bed. What an evening I had had. What delicious extravagance. My first opera, first supper, and a new friend. Life did yield wonderful surprises. The future was bright indeed. Before turning out the light I would just see what Theo's surname was. I laughed. As though it really mattered. I picked up the paper and unfolded it. The writing on it seemed familiar. I was struck by a terrible foreboding. I read the words: Jim Lees-Milne, 14 Onslow Gardens, S.W.7. It was my handwriting. My paper. I was dumbfounded.

I never found Theo again. I racked my brain for ways of getting into touch with him. I searched every likely place. For weeks I used to wait outside the Opera House when performances were about to begin. I stood in the Gallery the next time *Don Giovanni* was performed. I would hang around the entrance to the Café Royal, and wander upstairs scanning the tables. I have never so much as met anyone else called by his christian name. I do not even know if it was the diminutive of Theodore (meaning God's gift), or Theophilus (the loved of God). Theobald and Theodoric seem less fitting. I often wonder if I shall read in *The Times* list of deaths the entry of someone exactly my age whose first name is Theo. Perhaps he was run over and killed on the way home the evening we parted. Perhaps he did not survive the war. Did he emigrate? Is he by now a venerable patriarch with a grey beard? A retired bank manager growing chrysanthemums at Southend-on-Sea? A lonely squire in Flintshire, who on winter evenings strums Mozart arias on an old Broadwood piano? Perhaps he was a seraph after all. I rather wish I knew. But I am not absolutely certain that I do.

I still have his pencil. It is a little tarnished now, and has a curiously old-fashioned look.

VI

MAGDALEN TO MAFRA

HAVING COMPLETED the stenography and typewriting course with adequate credits I was again at a loose end. Not for the last time the question arose, what was I to do? Alas, no £5,000 a year directorship offered itself. My father was aghast. My mother, whose faith in me however severely tested remained unshakeable, was not quite so disappointed. She knew that I had always wanted to go to a university, and believed that it was the necessary culmination of every gentleman's education. A university must be even more important than a public school simply because the choice lay between two only, whereas Harrow, Winchester, Rugby and some few other public schools were not entirely ignoble alternatives to Eton. The single choice between Oxford or Cambridge was as imperative as that between a man's shoe- and gunmaker. The shoes came either from Lobb or Peel, the guns from Purdey or Holland and Holland. There was no other way of looking at these matters.

At this stage of my history my mother stepped firmly into the breach. She now happened to be at home, and my father to be away – not of course abroad, which he did not countenance unless it were Monte Carlo or Le Touquet for a fortnight in the spring. Since it was now August and the grouse season he was probably in Scotland. So my mother, with a determination which seized her when her emotions were aroused, declared that Oxford was to be my destination after all. She also declared that my father must pay for it. This was not unreasonable because she had little money of her own. The important thing was to fix everything up before his return. He must be faced with a *fait accompli* which he could not possibly revoke.

I went off on my motor scooter to be interviewed by the President of Magdalen College. Sir Herbert Warren had enjoyed the presidency for well over forty years. He was known to my mother whose brother had been at Magdalen under him. He received me graciously. I have met many obvious snobs in my life – in fact the majority of human beings, high and low, are snobs of one sort or another, which is what makes them so entertaining – but with the single exception of a restaurant proprietor in Moscow, I have never encountered a more blatant social snob than this eminent President. Mrs Roxburgh was a romantic snob who was fascinated by the vagaries of upper-class people. She even embroidered their eccentricities for fun. Sir Herbert honestly believed that a title conferred a heavenly grace in which those poor handleless creatures were sadly and totally lacking. How anyone without a title, and there were quite a few, ever got into Magdalen during Warren's presidency, I am at a loss to explain. That the titled and untitled were regarded by him as sheep and goats I am quite certain.

My mother who was aware of and amused by Sir Herbert's little foible primed me in advance. She had somehow managed to come upon a list of past and present members of Magdalen. Against those with illustrious prefixes she put a pencil tick. 'You must pretend,' she advised, 'that they are your relations. He will never find out.' 'But,' I protested, 'he's bound to. He's sure to have all their genealogies at his finger tips.' This did not turn out to be the case. My mother was right.

I was ushered into Sir Herbert's study. Oh, the horror of being interviewed! One feels like a cow in a market stall; a corpse on a dissecting table; a rabbit before a stoat: anything but a human being confronted by another human being. I was to undergo in the future far more alarming interviews than this particular one. Sir Herbert was not disagreeable. He did not set out to wither his victim with scathing satire. He did not expose the emptiness of my mind, or mock my intellectual pretensions. On the contrary he meant to put me at my ease. He merely cast an oblique aspersion upon my lineage.

It was easy to see that he had once been a large man. He was now crippled with arthritis, and lame. He had a pointed grey beard, authoritative lower lip – his least pleasant feature – and shrewd, yet kind eyes. He was very neatly dressed. He sat behind a knee-hole desk. He bowed me to a chair facing him. Immediately, with what I thought unnecessary carelessness, he allowed a large gold pen to slip from his fingers. In attempting to pick it up he dropped it on a woolly rug. 'Dear me!' he said, as I dived to retrieve it. 'Her Majesty's present which she gave me when His Royal Highness left the College.' Reverently I replaced it on his pen tray, which was an over-ornate adaptation in miniature of the Taj Mahal. I gave this vulgar object a quick glance of disparagement. 'I see,' he remarked, 'that you admire the Viceroy's little token.' 'O, rather!' I answered promptly. There was a pause. He then said, 'And how is your cousin Lord Fitzpatrick?' I was completely flummoxed, for I had never heard of such a person, nor was his name on my mother's list of fictitious relations. 'As far as I know, he is still flourishing,' I answered lamely. Suddenly I was inspired with self-confidence. If Sir Herbert Warren was capable of making such an inept mistake, I might risk deceiving him. 'But we all felt very sad, sir, when my great-uncle Evesham died,' I ventured. 'Evesham, Evesham,' he repeated, rolling the name round his tongue like a mouthful of non-vintage port. 'I don't recall him.' To my alarm Sir Herbert reached for the red book on the little table beside him, in order to jog his memory. 'I'm afraid you'll draw a blank there, sir,' I shouted desperately. 'There was no heir, sir. The title is now quite extinct.' Sir Herbert replaced the red book unopened, and grunted. I had had a narrow squeak. If after I left he consulted the *Extinct Peerage* and discovered my deception, he was too late. Perhaps he merely thought I was a fool and was confusing my home town with the title of another peer like, for instance, Lord Esher, who I regret to say was no relation whatever. At all events before I left he promised to take me, provided I passed the college entrance examination in six months' time. 'I do this,' he said with solemnity, 'for your uncle Robert's sake. He was one of Magdalen's best scholars. Only a demy, of course. Still he was a gentleman.' The last words were not uttered with that conviction which I would have liked. I accepted them as a delicate personal reproach.

Yet my mother and I were jubilant. She wrote immediately to Sir Herbert Warren asking him to confirm his promise in writing. He did so and his letter was in due course presented to my father on his return from the moors. Needless to say he was much displeased by our underhand machinations during his absence, and for committing him to the appalling expense of Oxford bills. Moreover he pointed out ominously that since he had last expressed his disapproval of Oxford University the number of niggers at Balliol had risen from three to five.

Sir Herbert retired from the presidency of Magdalen just before I matriculated, and went to live in the Woodstock Road. I used to have tea with him and Lady Warren in a little room made dark by Gothic windows and a monkey puzzle tree, whose branches were bare like the tails of mangy cats. In spite of my indifferent connections we remained friends. A fine scholar and a commendable poet in the Tennysonian style lay behind the arch-snob, for he was an essentially cultivated man. His last letter to me was written in 1930: 'I haven't seen you for a long time. Will you come again & see us and tell us about yourself, and about Lord Glenarthur & your cousin. I fear Lord G is very ill.' Lord G lived another twelve years. But before I could get to North Oxford Sir Herbert had died.

A few months of concentrated coaching ensued to prepare me for the College exam. This was provided by a well-known crammer, the Rev H. B. Allen who lived at Didbrook, a hamlet some twelve miles from my home. I used to ride there every day on my motor scooter. Allen, known to all as the Priest, was an eccentric clergyman of Rowlandson calibre. The editor of Lady Cynthia

Asquith's Diaries has summed him up in a sentence. 'Living to a very advanced age, he was a monument to the preservative powers of whisky and a firm believer in free love, and continued in a chronic state of insolvency because of the kindness of heart which led him to maintain a retinue of sick horses and donkeys.' For years he had been Vicar of Didbrook and Stanway, benefices in the patronage of Lord Wemyss. The Priest adored the Wemyss family and was adored by them in return. His duties resembled those of confidential chaplain to a nobleman's household of the eighteenth century rather than those of a twentieth-century country clergyman. He never bothered the parishioners in his cure, and was in consequence liked and respected by one and all. He and Mrs Allen, the Priestess, dined at Stanway at least once a week. Although the distance from Rectory to great house was not more than a mile and a half, the journey there and back called for much preparation and took a great deal of time. Their conveyance was an ancient tricycle. In hot or cold weather, summer or winter, the Priest twisted a thick woollen muffler two or three times round his neck. Wearing a wide-awake hat, long morning coat and outsize lambskin gloves, he mounted the machine at his front door. The Priestess then clambered up two steps behind her husband's saddle. Very stiff and upright she stood, brandishing a furled umbrella. After a good deal of pushing by the gardener-handyman, the resident pupils or any strong persons who happened to be about, the Priest began pedalling. Bent like a scythe over the handlebars, talking and laughing to himself, he slowly worked the pedals. Terrible occasions had been recorded when the ends of the Priest's muffler and the Priestess's umbrella had found their way into the wheel spokes, and brought them both crashing to the ground.

Hopelessly unpractical, improvident and vague, the Priest was a dedicated classical scholar with an ability to instill enthusiasm into his pupils. He saw the England of his day through the eyes of Theocritus, Virgil and Ovid, and the Cotswold valleys which he loved became the pastoral landscapes of classical Greece or Rome, peopled with bucolic shepherds piping to fleecy flocks, instead of lorry drivers careering down metalled roads with their fingers on the klaxon. He would sit on the window seat of his study with his arms round the neck of whichever pony happened to be grazing on the garden bed outside. In between kissing the pony's nose and stuffing its mouth with carrots he attended to us. Hesitant and giggling, slushing and adjusting his ill-fitting false teeth he would recite and translate for our benefit the Idylls, Eclogues and Metamorphoses from beginning to end. We were spellbound and fascinated by these recitations. They were truly inspiring, and the greatest fun. They taught us for the first time to appreciate the classics as living literature and history. They infused the ancient authors with new breath. But in imparting to us a mastery of the Latin and Greek languages the Priest was deficient. Mercifully the standard of college examinations was not then very high, and we succeeded in reaching it.

By 'we' I mean Johnnie Churchill and myself. For some reason the Priest's pupils had dwindled this summer to us two. Johnnie was the only boarder. He was almost as eccentric as the Priest. Like him he was totally detached from the present, and lived in an idealistic Valhalla of his own creation. All worldly concerns were dismissed by him with amused contempt. He was drawn equally to painting and music; talented in both and disciplined in neither. He had abundant good nature, outrageous animal spirits, and great physical strength and courage. He would appear out of the blue walking along the parapet of a roof on his hands, or standing on a chimney stack on one leg. Clad in a flowing Wagnerian cape and tricorne hat he would hold up the traffic in Cheltenham by giving a miming performance in the High Street. I remember him a year or so later similarly apparelled on the Ponte S. Angelo in Rome vehemently declaiming on the beauties of the river Tiber, regardless of the passers-by. A platoon of young blackshirts approached in rapid marching order. With his back turned to them and one wave of his strong right arm Johnnie knocked down the leading row of the platoon. They fell against the row behind them and in a trice the entire platoon was sprawling, one man on top of another, in the gutter. He had absolutely no respect for conventional behaviour, and took nothing seriously except his own artistic beliefs. My father regarded him as an unpredictable buffoon, whose antics might be masking subversive tendencies. For whenever he came to us over the weekend for tennis parties he treated the game, not as a sacred ritual but as a huge joke. At the same time he played better than anyone else which was, to say the least, vexatious for those, like my father, earnestly trying to excel.

Oxford for which I had so long clamoured turned out a bitter disappointment. I have always felt guilty towards my mother because I did not enjoy or profit from it more. She fought for me to go, and won the battle with my father, firmly believing that I would thereby justify her confidence in me. Although I did nothing to forfeit it, and left with a degree, I did not do anything remarkable to confirm it. I had looked forward to leading a cloistered existence in this mediaeval seat of learning. I imagined that my studies would be rigorously supervised, my tastes encouraged to expand, my intelligence cultivated and my steps guided by interested pastors and masters in the rook-racked, lichen-laden city. I longed to be taught, to be interested, and to learn. I would gladly have worked twelve hours a day and burnt the midnight oil, if only there had been supervision and encouragement. Instead the Oxford which I had mistakenly viewed through the eyes of my dead uncle of a generation ago had totally changed. The periphery was a hurly-burly of industrialism. Sir William Morris had ringed the city with factories and subtopia. To wander like the scholar-gipsy straight into the open country was no longer possible, even in 1928. In strolling round Addison's Walk or in Christ Church Meadow you were horribly aware of the rattle and din of traffic so that even in those backwaters quiet contemplation was out of the question. The High Street, Cornmarket, and indeed all the streets were jammed tight with lorries and cars, thrumming, hooting and belching exhaust fumes. Furthermore in those days Oxford absorbed an overflow of Mayfair good-timers. Except for the highly disciplined undergraduates whose circumstances withheld from them the wiles of social life, the prevailing spirit of frivolity was extremely disturbing.

I soon discovered that unless an undergraduate came to Oxford with outstanding academic recommendations the authorities paid not the slightest attention to him. They did not care a hoot whether he sank or swam. He would have no encouragement, no help. Tuition was minimal. His tutors were either too busy or too lazy to be bothered. So long as he attended the prescribed number of lectures he would not be penalized in any way. And who the hell can learn from lectures? To pass three hours a week feverishly trying to take down notes, or memorize a string of platitudes or paradoxes – usually the latter since most lecturers tend to show off – is utterly useless. A student does far better to read the stuff quietly in his room. It will take him a quarter of the time, and he will thus be able to concentrate without distractions. But he does need personal guidance as well.

One would suppose the purpose of a university to be to teach the unqualified who are anxious to be taught. I went to Oxford with few academic attainments. I left with no more. My three years at the University were a complete waste of time, a blank in my life over which I do not now care to linger. As it was, the term time only covered half the year. Six months out of every twelve one was down from Oxford, idling. What was the point of the whole institution? To make us men of the world? Eton had already started that process which the world itself, the world outside Oxford, was soon to complete. Few of my Eton friends went to Oxford, where I did not make many more. True, my extreme poverty was partially responsible. Although my father was committed to paying for my board and education, if such it was, he gave me no allowance. For pocket money I was once more dependent upon my mother's generosity and whim. Whereas poverty at school does not isolate a boy from his fellows, at Oxford and Cambridge in the Twenties and Thirties it ruled out most forms of social intercourse. I learned that the difference between having no private means and £200 a year of one's own was far greater than that between having £200 and £2,000.

The exclusiveness of the rich undergraduates and the cynicism of the dons were remarkable. Among the preceptors those who toadied to the *jeunesse dorée* to the neglect of the struggling scholars (among whom I cannot claim to be numbered) were probably the most intellectual in the University. The fact that the hungry sheep looked up and were not fed did not bother these tuft-hunting pedagogues. And needless to say, retribution from that two-handed engine at the door in the shape of a strong conscience was meaningless to men who propagated disbelief in all ethical values.

I will acknowledge that Oxford did two things for me. First, it aroused that love of architecture in which I have ever since been constant. Architecture which has brought me such immeasurable joy and pain. I do not suppose any adolescent susceptible to manmade beauty can spend a large part of three years at Oxford without being profoundly moved by those grey stones. In spite of the ceaseless nibbling at the city's green feet, in spite of the ever expanding 'base and brickish skirt', the industrial squalor, and the roar and stink of traffic, the university city is unsurpassed in the variety of distinguished buildings. I learnt at Oxford how of all the arts architecture is the only one which cannot be ignored either by the philistine or the indifferent. It is there. It cannot be avoided, and has to be seen. It must shape the minds and thoughts of all men whether they dislike or like it. In which case it is to the public's advantage to be good, and not bad. We cannot turn our backs upon it as we can upon painting, sculpture, and music, and pretend it does not concern or influence us – that we do not notice it. I also realized the terrible fragility of architecture. It is vulnerable to every insult, whether direct mutilation or indirect neglect, ignorant improvement, or environmental change.

One evening of a summer term, I was taken by friends to dine at Rousham on the river Cherwell midway between Oxford and Banbury. This remote Jacobean house was redecorated in about 1740 by William Kent, who likewise redesigned the landscape that encompassed it. The principal rooms with Kent's painted ceilings, stuccoed walls, marble chimney pieces, and gilt gesso furniture, and the collection of family portraits of Cottrells and Dormers, and other paintings, constitute an early Georgian monument of rare distinction. Kent's gardens with their temples, follies, terraces, grottoes and sculpture rank among the best preserved layouts of the period. The family who still own Rousham and are collateral descendants of its creator, had leased it to a capricious alcoholic. This individual who was rich, clever and slightly mad, had an irresistible appeal to sophisticated undergraduates. He had much to offer them, especially good food and a lot of drink. On this occasion we all dined exceedingly well. I, like the rest, made the most of what I was offered, and enjoyed myself thoroughly. But I did not get so drunk that I was not appalled by the meal's sequel. I was accustomed to Oxford evening orgies which were either boring or great fun, according to the mood one was in and the degree of one's successful participation in them. They were inevitably good natured and confined to one's contemporaries, or near contemporaries from London. This Rousham orgy was different. Our host seemed to me an old man. I suppose he was in his early thirties. He became noisy and rowdy. On leaving the dining room he got hold of a hunting crop, and cracked it against the portraits. With the thong he flaked off chunks of paint. When satisfied with working off some effects of his brandy on the Knellers and Reynoldses, he fetched a rifle from the gunroom. He went to the terrace and proceeded to fire at the private parts of the statues. I do not think that by then his aim can have been very accurate. For all I remember he missed, and I sincerely hope that the manhood of Apollo, Pan and the Dying Gladiator remains unscathed to this day. I have twice visited Rousham since, but on neither occasion could I bring myself to make a close inspection for fear of finding that some pudenda were missing, in which case I would hold myself partly responsible. For to my lasting shame I never raised a finger in protest against this hideous iconoclasm. Today no scruples of politeness or what a guest owed to his host would prevent me from hitting him until he desisted.

I was, it is true, only one among many, but that does not excuse, nothing ever does excuse pusillanimity. The other guests were vastly entertained. They cheered and egged on our beastly host in the way in which I am sure the sycophantic courtiers of Leo the Isaurian applauded that Emperor's overthrow of the Byzantine images. Not one of them betrayed by a flicker of the eye that he was faintly shocked. Yet all were fairly cultivated youths, and the don among the party was a man of letters who was to become a clamorous champion of western ideologies. At least I can truthfully say I did not cheer, but remained dumb. On the contrary I felt numb with dismay and misery. The experience was a turning point in my life. It brought home to me how passionately I cared for architecture and the continuity of history, of which it was the mouthpiece. I felt sick as many people would feel sick if they watched from a train window an adult torturing a child, while they were powerless to intervene. Those Rococo rooms at Rousham, with their delicate furniture, and portraits of bewigged, beribboned ancestors, were living, palpable children to me. They and the man-fashioned landscape outside were the England that mattered. I suddenly saw them as infinitely fragile and precious. They meant to me then, and have meant ever since, far more than human lives. They represent the things of the spirit. And the ghastly truth is that like humans, they are not perdurable.

That evening I made a vow – at the time it seemed so silly that I mentioned it to no one. I vowed that I would devote my energies and abilities, such as they were, to preserving the country houses of England. The opportunity was not to occur for at least six years. Thereafter I fulfilled my vow for three decades in, admittedly, a small way.

It could perhaps be argued that this revelation of the meaning of architecture which in my generosity I allow to Oxford might have come to me had I been living in some other city; and that Oxford does not provide the only route to Damascus. True perhaps, but it came while I was an undergraduate there, so Oxford may as well boast of having conferred the inestimable benefit. The second thing Oxford did for me – and beyond the two I can think of no others – was to arouse in me an implacable hatred of Communism. Hatred is deemed to be a great sin; but it can be a salutary emotion, a cleanser of the spirit. Hatred of human beings is a temptation – a great temptation – into which one ought not to fall. Hatred of animals and wild life is no temptation to me, and seems a worse sin. Hatred of things of beauty, which may be natural scenery and works of art, is the worst sin of all. It surely is the sin against the Holy Ghost, for which no retribution in this world or the next can be too severe. But hatred of false ideologies is a distinct virtue. One cannot love without hating, and without love one is not alive. So it is often one's bounden duty to hate.

The conduct of my contemporaries fanned the flames of my hatred of Communism. For while I was at Oxford many undergraduates were fellow travellers. Others became party members. These people belonged neither to the Bullingdon-Canterbury Quad set, nor to the impoverished scholar circles of Jesus and Brasenose. Neither the aristocracy nor the proletariat. Neither the aesthetes nor the hearties. They came from comfortable middle-class backgrounds. They were the intellectual élite of the University in the early thirties, who might be supposed to detect barbarism when they came upon it. Their potential superiority made a defection from the long tradition of European civilization all the more loathsome. In pretending to be the advocates of freedom of thought and improved conditions for the masses they favoured a creed (only the bravest dared adopt it openly) which for the past fifteen years they had seen to be the very negation of these ends in Russia. Throughout the thirties their communist proselytizing gathered strength and their activities became more and more pronounced. Although most of them have recanted long since (oh, yes, they nearly all survived the war), and their late middle-aged complexions are now faded to a bilious pink, the harm they did in their salad days was incalculable.

What made these particular intellectuals so contemptible was their dishonesty. They turned a blind eye upon the appalling mass murders, the persecutions unparalleled in history, the deliberate degradations of the individual, the debasement of standards of art and conduct which Communism had brought to the Soviet Union. Instead they screamed against the bestialities of Fascism and Nazism, which were not one jot more disgusting. If anything, existence for the ordinary citizen was preferable under a Fascist than under a Communist regime. At least under Fascism he was free to worship his God. Yet British intellectual leftists of the thirties threw themselves into the Spanish Civil War against Franco who was engaged in a life and death struggle with the forces of world disruption and anarchy. Their teaching is evident enough today among the proletarian intellectuals of the redbrick and plateglass universities where it has borne some putrid fruit. I hope that my leftist contemporaries occasionally ponder over what they have done, and suffer a little remorse for their past follies. Their fanaticism helped to contribute to the present-day falsification of political arguments, distortion of basic truths, and depreciation of civilized values.

During the General Election of 1931 I spent a fortnight at Stoke-on-Trent canvassing and bottle-washing in a humble capacity for Sir Oswald Mosley. I went under the aegis of his mother and staunch supporter. This excellent woman was the sister of my Aunt Dorothy, the relation to whom among the older generation I felt closest. At that date there was no hint that Tom Mosley would adopt Fascism. His New Party rallied a number of people who believed that it offered a solution to the mounting unemployment and despair of the working classes, and at the same time a substitute for Communism, which was being dangled like a succulent carrot in front of them by the intellectual leftists. My friends Christopher Hobhouse, just down from Oxford and barely twenty-one, Peter Howard and Harold Nicolson, whom I met during the campaign, contested constituencies. They were about the only reputable candidates. Quite a few M.Ps during the previous government had sympathized with Mosley's policy but backed out at the last moment. I now understand why. Although they admired

Mosley's ability, they mistrusted his judgment and suspected, not his sincerity, but his assessment of other men's character. As it turned out, they were right. If Mosley had had judgment he would have understood how grotesque the majority of his candidates were: a bruiser from Whitechapel, a sorry solicitor from the Midlands, a rugger-playing Buchmanite, a paradoxical under-graduate just out of his teens, and an ingenuous man of letters (albeit the noblest and best of men) were a cross-section of this motley army who knew less than nothing of the political game. Any other politician of Mosley's experience would have decided that unless more suitable candidates were attracted, it was better to pack up altogether and think afresh. Instead, because he failed to convert the country in one election he threw up the democratic sponge, and adopted Fascism, which was a bad and sad mistake.

As the campaign proceeded I became more and more uneasy. From my very subordinate position I watched Mosley closely. It became clear that he was in those days righteous in his own esteem. He did not know the meaning of compromise. He brooked no argu-ment, would accept no advice. He was overbearing and over-confident. He had in him the stuff of which zealots are made. His eyes flashed fire, dilated and contracted like a mesmerist's. His voice rose and fell in hypnotic cadences. He was the slave of his own rhetoric. It might be a terrible day, I fancied, were it to run away with him and take a blind turning. The posturing, the grimacing, the switching on and off of those gleaming teeth, and the overall play-acting, so purposeful and calculated, were more likely to seduce Mayfair flappers than to sway indigent workers in the Potteries. I did not then, and do not now, think that the art of coquetry ought to be introduced into politics.

I believe that Mosley is no longer like this. He has acquired a tolerance and wisdom which, had he only displayed them forty years ago, could have made him into a great moral leader. Few of us are what we were. It is a pity that he was not then what he has now become too late. He is a man of great brilliance and unusual per-spicacity, but because some of his strong convictions are slightly off beam his every utterance is a target for wilful misrepresentation and abuse.

Having finally gone down from Oxford in 1931 I was again without a job, and no nearer knowing what I ought to do. What I wanted to do I had to keep to myself, because it was quite irreconcilable with earning a living. By now my father had completely washed his hands of me. I do not blame him. He argued that I had received the most expensive education known to man, and if I were still not equipped for the world that was my fault. My B.A. degree was no help whatever. It never has been. No one has ever asked me whether I got a degree, or what class it was. To become a fully fledged M.A. involved paying £10 for the privilege. I could not afford the hollow luxury. After a month or two of perplexity while staying with an adopted aunt in Northamptonshire I remembered my rusty qualifications as stenographer and typist. I entered myself on a London agent's list and feverishly took to my pencil and typewriter.

The first name I was given was that of a distinguished proconsul who had been Governor of Bombay and High Commissioner in Egypt. He was back in England without office, but busily engaged in politics, active in the House of Lords and chairman of several important societies and companies. Lord Lloyd of Dolobran was in need of a typist. I was given particulars by the agency and told to present myself at 9.20 one morning. I donned my suit. On arrival at a large Georgian house in Portman Square (a house of much architectural merit and so, of course, recently demolished) a footman in a striped waistcoat and with a disdainful nose signalled me into the one empty hall chair out of six, telling me to wait my turn. On the five other chairs were perched in a row against the wall five strikingly plain and pinched ladies, who were also applicants (I afterwards learned that the agency had expressly selected them for their looks owing to Lord Lloyd's terror of being vamped). This was discouraging. For twenty minutes we sat upright in painful silence. It was only broken by the ticking of a large table clock and an occasional snivel

– it was mid-winter – from the ladies. At last the footman returned and ushered us one by one into his lordship's library.

I was the last to be interviewed. As the footman closed the door softly behind me I saw a dapper figure with his back bent over a large writing-table in the window, fumbling through papers. I waited respectfully at a distance, examining the dark, immaculately groomed hair which was thinning. Without turning round the figure growled: 'Well, now, Miss – er, I'm afraid I'm already satisfied.' There was a pause. Was I meant to withdraw? Instead I said sadly, 'What a pity, sir.' The figure swivelled round rapidly in its chair, and barked: 'Who on earth are you? What are you doing here?' I apologized for my presence, and my sex. I then explained that I too was an applicant. Lord Lloyd's demeanour changed instantly from the proconsular to the natural. He smiled very engagingly and became almost boyish. He fired off a hundred direct questions without waiting for an answer to any of them. He gave me a fascinating dissertation on the flabbiness of the National Government, about which I was very ignorant. He talked about religion, of which I knew rather more. This subject and a mutual detestation of Communism were our bond. The upshot of the interview was that he engaged me, not I fancy without some misgiving, and almost as a joke. It was almost inconceivable to him that a man could do shorthand and typewriting, and be capable of drafting letters and speeches. He was ready to experiment with such a phenomenon.

I stayed with him for three and a half years. He was an exacting taskmaster and disciplinarian, for which I am immensely beholden to him. From the start I feared and liked him. In the end I was devoted to him. I was never entirely in sympathy with his brand of imperialism which seemed to me out of date, nor with his opposition to self-government for India which seemed to me inevitable. I loved the poet and mystic in him. His sheer goodness and companionableness were irresistible.

When the interview was over I went straight to the nearest public library and looked up Lord Lloyd in *Who's Who*. Until that morning I had had practically no idea who he was. I began work next morning at nine o'clock sharp. There was an embarrassing encounter in the hall with the lady typist whom Lord Lloyd had engaged before he saw me. She, poor thing, was indignant to be told by the snooty footman that she was not wanted after all. I have been haunted ever since by her hurt expression. There is nothing in life more pathetic than the wounded pride of little people, especially women, little or big.

Regularly thereafter I would begin work shortly before nine o'clock each morning. My first task which was to sort through my employer's papers and evolve a schedule for his day's, and indeed week's engagements ahead, remains in my memory more vividly than any other. It necessitated haste before he finished breakfast in the dining room beyond the library. Today I cannot hear the distant, indistinct rise and rumble to a high key, followed by the low monotone of two men talking and laughing in an adjoining room without recalling those early mornings in Portman Square. The experience at once fills me with a delicious unease, and spurs me to some unwonted activity. For Lord Lloyd usually had a friend to breakfast with him. It might be Sir Roger Keyes, Noël Coward, or (self-invited) T. E. Lawrence, that gnome-like creature with a gnome's chin and prominent boots, who saw his friends at hours of his own choosing. Breakfast was one of the rare half-hours of Lloyd's working days (which numbered 360 out of the 365) when he allowed himself the companionship of his intimates. I believe he never slept more than four hours at night. Before rising he had already digested *The Times* and *Morning Post*, and his enormous mail from home and overseas. By 8.45 he was fully equipped for argumentative combat with the privileged guest at a disadvantage from having come a distance, and from being possibly a less early riser than himself. This he never appreciated. He would ask for comments on the *Morning Post* leader, or some inconspicuous letter on Sir Jamsetjee Jejeebhoy's interpretation of the Indian Legislative Assembly's functions, expressing aggrieved surprise if the pith of it had escaped the other's notice.

These breakfasts, delightful and stimulating as they were – and many was I to enjoy after I had left him – were nothing like so rewarding as those occasions far into the night when business was finally set aside. He would then thrust that compact, tight little body which never properly belonged to him, however adorned and cared for, but was treated as a convenient machine like his expensive two-seater, and driven to the last ounce of his inner energy, into the corner of a deep sofa, and talk and talk of his soul's problems and aspirations until the small hours. Over a large tumbler of whisky and soda, which was the only alcohol this ascetic man allowed himself, the endearing character of George Lloyd was revealed, and the anagogical labours of his tortured psyche were partially disclosed. So precious and confidential were the talks I had with him far into the night that I cannot trust myself to refer to them here in any detail.

St. Paul in his Epistle to the Galatians says: 'Walk in the spirit and you shall not fulfil the lusts of the flesh.' Few of us can accept this injunction. Lloyd did. 'Caro enim concupiscit adversus spiritum.' Then in the next breath the saint shows his worldly wisdom, for he goes on: 'Spiritus autem adversus carnem, for these are contrary one to another, so that you cannot do the things that you would.' George Lloyd persistently allowed his spirit to sin against his flesh.

But at those intimate breakfasts from which only he truly profited, sipping abstemiously from an orange and sucking, draining out matter from the sleepy cells of the other's languid brain, swallowing what he wanted (in that respect he never went empty) and throwing away the rind, even he was not thoroughly at ease. Ever anxious to have done with the meal and project himself upon the day's papers on his writing-table which I this while was frantically disentangling and setting in order, he would flit about the dining room, swing his eye-glass on its thin black cord, run it through his fingers to his lips, and playfully bite the gold rim for a moment until he laughed and let it fall. He would shove back his chair, pounce upon the sideboard, peer into the sausages, sniff the scrambled eggs, then leaving off the covers abuse the cook, the butler, footman and valet in one breathless, good-natured malediction, all in a lightning, bird-like movement, without once stopping to consider that he did not allow enough time for his guest to eat and follow the train of his questions simultaneously.

Without doubt the tragedy of Lloyd's career to my mind was his hallucination that he was everlastingly pursued by the furious Erinyes in retribution for opportunities lost, and hours misspent on false anagogical trails; an hallucination that the shears of Atropos were hot on his heel, and that the faster he ran from them, the further they would keep their distance. Moreover I fear he never quite made up his mind what the Grail was for which he so passionately yearned – self-fulfilment? imperial glory? the betterment of mankind? union with God? – and which, distracted by countless conflicting, psychic will-o'-the-wisps, he surely did not ultimately attain. If only he could have slackened the frenetic search and chase, the exhaustion of which prematurely killed him. Did he, I have often asked myself, realize at the end what a confused merry-go-round his life had been – a ceaseless flight from what, and pursuit of what?

Lord Lloyd did not reach the dizziest heights of public service (in the war he became Secretary of State for the Colonies and leader of the House of Lords). His conservatism was held to be a little reactionary. But his views were respected by friends and foes alike, and his speeches were listened to, if not always heeded. He was probably held in higher esteem on the continent than at home. Heads of state never refused to see him when he asked for an audience in passing through a foreign capital. He met Mussolini and Hitler several times and never shrank from telling them exactly what impression they were making on the British parliament and people. He was an effective, if self-appointed plenipotentiary whom foreigners understood, if they did not always like. He represented to them the latent resilience and strength of a Britain which had not declined since the Diamond Jubilee nor ebbed away with the blood spilled on Flanders' fields. Lloyd's harsh, outspoken voice was a reminder to the strutting mountebank dictators and the democratic Prime Ministers of European states that Great Britain might not be quite so decadent as Oxford Union resolutions led them to suppose.

The admiration in which Lord Lloyd's name was held abroad was strongly impressed upon me by an embarrassing incident which occurred in 1932. In August of that year I went for a month's holiday to the north of Spain and Portugal. I think the whole expedition cost me £25. I travelled by train, sitting at nights bolt upright on the narrow wooden bench of a third-class railway compartment, wedged between orange-sucking and garlic-chewing peasants, who balanced on their knees miniature trunks of wicker-work, bundles tied with cord and wire cages filled with linnets. When not snoring on my shoulder they were swigging sour wine from the necks of bottles. Santiago da Compostella was the first goal of my pilgrimage. From there I proceeded in slow stages by antiquated country buses across the Portuguese frontier down to Lisbon. In those days the Portuguese country was little known to foreigners. There was only one railway from north to south, the roads were extremely rough, narrow and dusty, the inns primitive ('poor' was the invariable description given by Baedeker) and the food dull and unwholesome. All the country people wore a picturesque national dress, of which the hats both male and female varied in each province from woollen bonnets with bobbles to felt pancakes with poms. I did not meet a single working Portuguese who was not helpful and friendly, including the touts of the inferior hotels I frequented, 'the splendour of whose gold-laced caps' (Baedeker warned) 'is a very fallacious index to the comforts of the hostelries they represent.'

In Lisbon I attended a cocktail party given by a member of the British Embassy staff. This entailed wearing the only tidy suit which my exiguous hand luggage contained. I was soon introduced to a very old and indescribably distinguished gentleman in uniform of scarlet and gold. His shoulders were padded with epaulettes the size of brickbats. His jacket was frogged, piped and braided. Rows of medals and stars adorned his chest. Blue and yellow ribbons entwined his neck and waist. Beside him on the floor was a vast helmet with a stiff peak of patent leather trimmed with gold galloon. From the crown a fountain of plumes and feathers dyed orange and purple sprouted 2½ feet into the air and cascaded over the carpet. The Commander-in-Chief of the Portuguese Forces spoke very indifferent English, was exceedingly deaf, and possibly a little blind. My name of course meant nothing to him at all. At first this splendid person was understandably bored by having his attention distracted from some glamorous female and directed upon a callow English youth. But my host was persistent. 'He is secretary,' he twice repeated while pointing at me, 'to Lord Lloyd.' ''Oo ees 'e?' the Commander-in-Chief demanded with remarkable lack of interest. 'To Lord Lloyd, whom you admire so much,' my host bawled again into his ear. The penny dropped, more or less accurately. 'Lor Lloy!' he echoed, and the old eyes momentarily lost their glaze and emitted a sparkle of comprehension. The broad chest heaved. The silver medals rattled a response. And from the depths of that military bosom disjointed phrases of intense regard erupted in broken English.

For five minutes an awkward tête-à-tête ensued. The Commander-in-Chief was amazingly affable, I almost wrote deferential. He begged me to give him my views on the European situation and dared to hope that, in the event of Portugal being attacked by the Canary Islands, I would guarantee Great Britain's immediate assistance to her oldest ally by way of two divisions at least. Mercifully he was unable to hear, or understand, my laboured replies. He seemed fairly satisfied however with the sweet smile of sympathy which I managed to assume. He then asked me how long I was staying in Lisbon, where I was going to next, and what he could possibly do to make my stay agreeable. He craved permission to confer upon me some signal favour. I was immensely flattered but not a little surprised by his sudden eagerness to please. There was nothing, I assured him, that I was in need of. I was in fact leaving Lisbon very shortly for home. It is true that tomorrow I intended going to Mafra for the day. I was anxious to visit the Escorial of Portugal. Did the Commander-in-Chief happen to know whether the whole of the monastery-palace was open to visitors, or merely the church? I really asked this banal question in order to get away from Canary-Portuguese relations, which I felt might lead me into deep waters. Having repeated it three times I regretted ever having raised it. After all, what possible interest could the architecture of Mafra have for this dreary old soldier? At last he understood. 'Mafra', he replied possessively, 'has nine courtyards, 700 rooms, 2,500 windows and 5,200 doors. Every single room will be open to your Excellency. And what time will your Excellency arrive at Mafra?' he asked. 'Oh! round about eleven o'clock,' I said brightly. 'Very well,' he said, 'I will have everything arranged. Present this' – and he handed me a flamboyantly engraved, gilt-edged card, 'to the officer in command. Good-bye, your Excellency. *Enchanté*.' And he clicked his heels, bowing graciously from the waist. I did the same. Really, the courtesy of these foreigners, I murmured to myself.

'You were a great success,' my host said as I left the party. 'I've never known the old boy be so unbending. He's usually insufferably arrogant with the young.'

The next morning I put on again my old, travel-stained flannel trousers and un-matching, crumpled jacket. It was going to be a grilling day. I wore an open-necked shirt and sandshoes over sockless feet. Since I was not going to be in Lisbon – and in those days one wore a suit and tie in a capital city even in August – my shabby clothes would not matter. I took a crowded bus for the twenty-five-mile drive to Mafra where the peasants, their livestock and I were spewed, sweating and panting, on to the Praça da República. Straight ahead the unbroken front of the monastery-palace stretched 823 feet from one square pavilion to another. Between two imposing entrances rose the central twin towers and dome of the church. Not a tree, not an awning offered shade from the pitiless sun now high in the heavens. I made a dash for shelter under the portico. It was already eleven o'clock. I reckoned that I had one hour before church and public rooms shut at midday. It would be agreeable, I decided, to look at these at leisure by myself. I would then, if I felt like it, present my friend's card at the right-hand entrance where I noticed two sentries to be standing. That side of the building was presumably the barracks.

So I took my time enjoying the variegated marbles of the nave, the white Carrara statues of saints and evangelists, and the stucco bas-reliefs of Annunciation and Assumption. I passed into the sacristy, the monks' pharmacy and refectory. Next I climbed to the first floor and visited the royal family's apartments, and the immense Rococo library. At twelve o'clock to the accompaniment of church bells and cannon I found myself on the *praça* again. Now did I, or did I not want to see any more of the building before lunching? I had really had my fill, and it was stiflingly hot. But it seemed a pity not to make use of privilege when it came one's way. Yes, I would after all ask an officer to show me those rooms worth seeing to which the public did not have admittance.

I approached the entrance to the barracks. Both sentries leapt to attention and barred my passage aggressively. I waved in their faces the Commander-in-Chief's magnificent card, and was about to explain what I wanted when their attitude instantly changed. One of them, emitting a low whistle, dashed to the guardroom switchboard, and began pressing buttons and telephoning. Within two minutes a clean-shaven young Captain appeared at a smart trot, followed by a slightly older Major frowning over a waxed moustache. They were resplendent in full dress uniform, snow-white breeches, glistening top boots with spurs, and plumed casques. For a fleeting second the young Captain hesitated before the scruffy apparition confronting him. But with the true soldier's admirable self-command immediately recovered himself. 'Lor Lloy!' he exclaimed aloud, and to himself no doubt, 'I have always heard these English are a race of damned eccentrics.' Before I had time to disabuse him he introduced himself as O Capitão Cavalheiro Xavier de Marialva. 'Allow me,' he said, 'to present to your Excellency the second-in-command here, my superior officer,

Major O Conde Nuno da São Vicente e Linhares.' I proffered a limp hand. The Major clicked his heels, perceptibly curled his lip under his moustache, and wrung my hand in a vice-like grip.

'The Conde da São Vicente e Linhares speaks no English,' the Captain resumed. 'No one here speaks any English, except myself. I speak much English, but I do not understand it – not one word.' He was certainly voluble, and friendly. 'The Colonel he wait for you since eleven o'clock. Very hot morning. The men faint.' He gave a watery smile. The Major looked reproachful. 'Excuse me, Excellency, we must hurry.' The two of them rushed me down vaulted corridors, through courtyards, under arches, and into extensive cloister walks round a garden of low box hedges and a mossy fountain. I was now seriously alarmed. The ghastly mistake had only just dawned on me. What was yet in store for me I dared not guess. There was absolutely no way of escape. Expostulation was clearly useless. On and on we went. I felt sick at heart. I thought my legs must come apart from my knees. The Major and the Captain's snow white breeches twinkled ahead. Their spurs jingled rhythmically upon the flagstones. Automatically I fell into step with their striding black boots. We left the cloisters and passed through yet another wide passageway between the deserted monks' cells and below the library. Suddenly we were precipitated into a vast open training ground of gravel and dust. The glare was almost blinding. The heat beat down from an opaque sky and radiated back as from an oven. To my dismay I discerned in front of us a regiment lined up in irreproachable regular ranks.

Upon our emergence from the palace there was a quick roll of drums and the men were brought abruptly to attention. 'This way, Excellency.' The Major and the Captain directed me to a little group standing apart on a wooden dais. I was marched up some carpeted steps, and a further, more solemn presentation took place this time under 2,000 astonished pairs of eyes. If only I had been wearing my suit, I thought in agony, the situation would be a degree less appalling than it was. 'Sua Excelência, O Coronel Dom Vergilio, Marquez de Belém e Setúbal e Bragança – Sua

Excelência, Lor Lloy!' bawled the Captain. The Colonel and his six A.D.Cs, the Major and the Captain drew themselves to their full height, which I was gratified to observe was less than mine, and saluted me with wonderful precision. Nervously I acknowledged this military greeting by raising a hand to my sweating forehead. Whereupon with great condescension the Colonel tickled me on both cheeks with his long and bristly moustache in full view of the troops.

Before I had time to consider what I was expected to do next there was another prolonged roll of drums, and the regimental band struck up. I took some minutes to recognize that the tune was God Save the King played extremely slowly and throughout its full three verses. It was followed by what I took to be the Portuguese national anthem, which was no more abbreviated. From my vantage point I was concerned to see quite a dozen soldiers – the regiment had been standing in the blazing sun for an hour and a quarter on my account – fall stiffly to the ground like ninepins, without a groan.

These preliminaries over, the Colonel indicated that I must descend from the scaffold. The party followed suit. 'Your Excellency,' the Captain explained blandly, 'will now inspect the Army of the Republic. Coronel O Marquez de Belém e Setúbal e Bragança begs your Excellency to be unsparing with your criticisms.' This was a highly disconcerting exhortation which for some time I ignored. Slowly and deliberately we went the rounds, myself in the van, the Colonel a discreet pace behind, then the Major, the Captain, the six A.D.Cs and a handful of N.C.Os who had tagged on to the rear. I pretended to scrutinize the troops. If I threw so much as a glance at a man the N.C.Os closed in on him like the shadows of death. The silence and the heat were increasingly oppressive. The only interruptions were further falls of ninepins. I am sorry to say I welcomed them as distractions from my predicament. I sensed however that my hosts would soon be disappointed, and contemptuous, if I did nothing to break the monotony of approval. I felt honour bound to find fault with someone. Desperately I halted in front of one luckless soldier, chosen at random, and peered myopically at his buttons. As far as I could see they shone no less brilliantly than those of his fellows. Still I could not bring myself to utter a rebuke. I had however done enough. The angels of death swooped upon him. A corporal seized him by the collar and shook him. 'Sujo! Filthy!' a sergeant shouted at him. 'Porco!' He was dragged away, and to the cries of 'Desgraça! Desgraça!' driven at the bayonet point off the parade ground. Poor fellow, he was, I fear, incarcerated in solitary confinement on bread and water, for at least a week. I felt terribly guilty. I had exonerated myself at this innocent soldier's expense. Perhaps I had ruined his chances of future promotion, for ever.

I will dwell no further on this humiliating visit to Mafra. When at last the inspection was over and the regiment dismissed we retired to the officers' mess where I was regaled with food and drink. The Captain remained fairly cordial. So did some of the junior officers who were not averse to a little comic relief. But the Major and the Colonel were distinctly stuffy. I knew better than to ask now to see any private rooms of the palace. In fact I was longing to get away as soon as I decently could. My worry was how to do so, for I knew the only afternoon bus back to Lisbon had left. When the time for my departure was clearly indicated a shamefaced A.D.C. whispered to the Captain that nowhere could his Excellency's chauffeur be found. I could only protest: 'How extraordinary! Where can he have got to? Perhaps he misunderstood and went home.' Eventually a military escort was summoned. I was driven away in a motor with a flag on its bonnet, and deposited at my pension in a back street of Lisbon.

I was so unnerved by the Mafra incident that I left the capital next morning. For several weeks after my return to London I went in dread lest a letter should arrive from our Embassy in Lisbon complaining that I had carried out a hoax in extremely poor taste upon the Portuguese army. Luckily Lord Lloyd never found out. I very much doubt whether he would have been amused.

VII

BANDITS AND BEASTS

FOR THREE and a half years I remained private secretary to
Lord Lloyd. Now the first forty years of my uneventful life
fell – and the further back they recede the more clearly are
they seen by me – into periods of contrasting ups and downs. Those
with Lord Lloyd were a distinct 'up' period. They were crammed
with interest, experience and hard work, which has always agreed
with me. Lloyd was consistently long-suffering and generous.
From the start he took it for granted that I was going to be a satisfactory secretary. This risky assumption had the effect of making
me more efficient than it was really in my nature to be. He gave me
his unreserved confidence, which won my boundless loyalty. He
introduced me to people I would otherwise never have met, many
who became friends of a lifetime, some who were but fleeting
meteors, like T. E. Lawrence, Rudyard Kipling and the enigmatical
Ribbentrop. Lord Lloyd saw through and cordially disliked this
Prussian vintner from the moment he was sent to London as
Hitler's special envoy, and long before he became German
Ambassador. I can never forget Ribbentrop's endeavour to explain
to him at luncheon in Portman Square the poor Führer's distress at
being obliged to shoot his best friend Röhm, during the Night of
the Long Knives in June of 1934, so that for quite six hours afterwards he lost all appetite for food; nor the look of intense disgust on
Lloyd's face before he exploded in violent denunciation of the
whole barbaric business. 'May we hope,' Lloyd barked, with an

irony which was totally wasted on this obtuse animal, 'that the Führer may also have lost, once and for all, his appetite for blood?'

In August and September of 1933 I again went abroad by myself for a holiday which Lloyd, out of the goodness of his heart, paid for. This time I chose Corsica, crossing the Mediterranean by boat from Nice to Bastia, thence by crawling train to Calvi. Here I stayed in a modern hotel below the old town which was perched on a citadel overlooking the wide bay. Calvi could not have changed much since 1794 when Nelson lost his right eye during its siege by British troops. There were then few buildings outside the old citadel. The hotel stood close to the beach, which was thronged all day long with fishermen dragging in nets of sardines, idling half on land, half in the water, and tending their boats. From one of these amphibious creatures, by name Dominique, I hired his boat and services. By night I would accompany him into the bay where we fished with the aid of a powerful acetylene lamp. By day I used his upturned boat in which to keep my books and clothes while I was bathing. It also served as the only available shade against the pitiless sun. Dominique, who apart from a little desultory fishing seemed to have nothing whatever to do, became a self-appointed slave. I soon learned that like all Corsicans he was intensely possessive and jealous. He made it abundantly clear that once I had hired his boat I might never hire anyone else's. And when one morning on leaving the hotel I was accosted by another youth who recommended the superior qualities of his boat, trouble broke out. Dominique appeared like a djinn from thin air, upbraided me with the most menacing gestures in a torrent of Corsican patois and gave chase to the would-be rival with a long curved knife. Thereafter, I heeded this equivocal warning. The knife became an appalling bore. At the smallest provocation, the hint of a criticism, the suspicion of a slight, an unfavourable comparison with another youth, it was unsheathed and brandished in the air, accompanied by a threat that it would be used upon his own throat, not mine. I was never quite convinced how disingenuous his suicidal protestations were. I suspected that no scruples would have prevented him from plunging that knife into the throat of any human being, including me, who happened to incense him beyond the narrow limits of his endurance. In fact he confessed to me later that he had already done so more than once.

I have never been greatly given to beachcombing. After ten days of bathing and lying naked in the sun at Calvi I grew restless. It is true I made friends. Robert Sherard and his wife were among them. They lived in extreme indigence in the old town. He was then over seventy and spent his declining days and money pathetically printing pamphlets in refutation of 'the odious charges brought against my old friend by Shaw, Harris and Gide', as he wrote to me after I got back to England. For he had been Oscar Wilde's first biographer. Wilde in prison referred to his 'fine, chivalrous friendship', but in later years became embarrassed by his protagonist's battles with pen, and also fists, on his behalf. Sherard likewise defended, and befriended, the poet Ernest Dowson, who died in his house in 1900. He was a noble, quixotic and rather dotty man. Infuriated by the Oxford pacifists he wrote in the same letter from which I have just quoted, about a proposal he was putting forward to the Government. 'I consider them a disgrace to England and suggest that as most Oxford undergraduates . . . derive their social status from land granted to their ancestors by the King, they should, if unwilling to carry out the conditions under which the feoffments were made to them by the Crown (which was that of military service), return to the Crown these lands if still in the possession of their families; or if they owe their wealth to money obtained by their families from the sale of these lands at any time in their family history, the value of these lands should be sent by postal order to the Chancellor of the Exchequer.'

Calvi was at this time a place where the flotsam and jetsam of Russian émigrés were washed up. I think many of these cultivated and tragic exiles were dependent for subsistence upon Prince Félix Yussoupov, who had a villa nearby and some money he had managed to escape with out of Russia. There was Count Cheremetew, a most distinguished old gentleman, who sold lottery tickets at the equivalent of 2d each as a desperate alternative to starving to death in a garret. Every evening Prince Yussoupov and his friends forgathered at the Napoleon Bar. The proprietor of this bistro was an Englishman engaged to a Corsican girl whose brother hovered around with a revolver which he threatened to let off if the nuptials were not celebrated by a stipulated date. I never missed an evening drinking and gossiping with the Russian émigrés, and listening to their fantastic tales about the bandits who were then still flourishing in the island, and defying every effort of the authorities to round them up. They were eventually rounded up by the Army less than two years later when the chief bandit, André Spada, who had twenty-one outrageous murders to his credit, was captured and guillotined. Spada was in 1933 held by all Corsicans in absolute dread and awe. His name was only mentioned among groups of trusted friends in nervous whispers. Most Corsicans turned a blind eye and a deaf ear to banditry in case they might unwittingly become involved in a vendetta, which was liable to spread its tentacles to embrace whole communities. As a rule a vendetta was confined to families, and at most clans, the membership of which was sometimes not easily definable. The terrible thing was that vengeance might never die. One evening while I was talking to the Sherards in the old town a shot rang out in a nearby alley. They told me next day that an old Corsican who had left the island for America thirty years before and just returned on a short visit to his relations was picked off in retaliation for a murder committed by a cousin long before the First War.

The usual course of events was that one man might for a trivial reason, and in a momentary quarrel, murder another and take to the mountains rather than face trial. In any case the penalty was seldom more than five years' imprisonment, and often merely two. A member of the victim's family would track down the murderer and dispatch him or, if it was easier, his brother or first cousin. He in turn would disappear inland. Once started a vendetta could last for generations. It would be deliberately fomented as the years passed. For instance, a piece of the original victim's blood-stained clothing would be handed down in a family, and venerated as a sacred relic.

The descendants would reverently kiss it and renew oaths of vengeance over it. The vendetta might only peter out with the death by violence of the last survivor of a family. Until a whole family was exterminated members of the rival family often did not have a care-free moment, and moved in terror of their lives. Even then the vendetta could be carried on by the clan. Meanwhile the assassins took to life on the run, married and begat children, who became hereditary bandits. Sometimes several generations never knew any other existence than that of shifting from one cave or hiding-place to another. Members of vendettas well knew and respected the ter-ritory of rivals, and took good care not to trespass upon it.

I was fascinated by the tales of these strange people and by the bandit lore. For the bandits observed a strict moral code of their own. In the first place they never molested foreigners who did not interfere with them. On the contrary it was a point of honour to assist them if they came upon them in the maquis. They would take upon themselves the rôle of protective police in areas which the *gendarmerie* dared not penetrate. They would administer their own law and order of a summary kind. They would banish petty thieves and robbers from the areas they controlled. They would carry out capital punishment in other cases of crime. They would dispense money to the poor and help people in distress. They were not given to indiscriminate robbery themselves. Their robbery was carefully selective. It was directed against rival clans or persons whom they deemed rich enough, or disagreeable enough, to deserve mulcting.

I learned these particulars from the Russians who after a few absinthes would talk very freely and indiscreetly about the bandits. Prince Yussoupov was specially attracted to them, which was not altogether surprising since he had once behaved like one. No Corsican however joined in these talks, and those who happened to be sitting at neighbouring tables would, I noticed, slink unobtru-sively away. Not so Dominique. This Don Dismallo would always be within hearing, lugubriously mending a net on the sand a few feet below the bistro, or sharpening that ghastly knife while he squatted beside our table. No amount of drinks would elicit a word from him on the subject. Occasionally he raised his head when he overheard a remark of which he disapproved, and scowled darkly.

One night while sitting in the stern of Dominique's boat far out in the bay, and watching the gnats and mosquitoes which even away from the land seemed more attracted to the acetylene lamp than the fish were, I asked him outright to talk to me about the bandits. 'Shut up!' he growled. 'Your voice carries across the sea.' He anxiously looked over a mile of ultramarine water towards the black hump of the citadel and the flickering lights of old Calvi. There was not a sound beyond the lapping of wavelets, like a pack of puppies' tongues against the hull. I thought his anxiety exaggerated. 'I merely wanted to learn,' I said injuredly, 'if you knew any bandits, and could introduce me to some.' This remark provoked a lunge at me with the oar which nearly capsized the boat. 'You are impossible. One does not ask such questions. One is more cautious. One is discreet. One minds one's business. One does this. One doesn't do that. But like all foreigners you are mad,' he said.

The long and the short of this outburst was that before the night was ended Dominique had confessed to me under seal of strictest secrecy, which necessitated drawing blood with the point of his dagger from his thumb and mine and mingling the drops, just like two boy scouts, that he was a bandit, the son and the grandson of bandits. He explained that he spent far the greater part of the year in the maquis with his parents, brothers, sisters and cousins, and only came down to the coast in the summer months to pick up whatever crumbs might fall from the rich tourists' tables. He had received no education whatever, and had never yet slept in a proper bed, or even house. When at Calvi he merely dossed in or under his boat. He had no idea how old he was. Time, religion, truth, material ambition meant nothing to this splendid animal; loyalty and vengeance everything. His family were the sworn partisans of Spada, who was king, god, and the star around which life revolved. The Bonelli family on the other hand were the fiends incarnate, the total extinction of whose every member – and they were legion – was life's single purpose. Spada the source and giver of every virtue: the Bonelli the absolute negation of good and epitome of evil. How simple it all was and, when one could discount the bloodshed, what fun vendettas were. The whole of Corsican politics was, I understood, a glorious game, rather like French-and-English in nursery days.

Before we rowed back to Calvi at dawn Dominique, who vowed he could deny me nothing, undertook to introduce me to his king and god. But he emphasized the appalling risk he ran from the Bonelli who were lurking behind every doorpost in Calvi – had I not heard the gunshot last Wednesday evening? I had – and every tuft of scrub in the maquis. I was again sworn to secrecy – this time without bloodletting for we were practically at the quay – the betrayal of which (to whom? I couldn't help interjecting) would oblige him, much against his will, to slit himself, not me of course, instantly from one ear to the other. To emphasize this cruel necessity the knife blade was whipped out for me to feel its edge. 'Tell me, Dominique,' I asked, as I eagerly jumped ashore, 'how many Bonelli have you assassinated with this lovely instrument?' 'Only two, so far,' he answered rather sadly, 'but just wait till I get my revolver. You *will* help me to buy one, won't you?' The innocence of this little-boy request for a new toy was undeniably appealing.

Dominique was as good as his word. I knew he would be. He arranged the whole expedition, which went like clockwork. The two of us left Calvi the next day, on foot, after dark, so that our departure should not be noticed by the Bonelli. A mile outside the town we mounted two mules. These animals are the only positively malevolent breed I have yet encountered, and utterly uncooperative if you want them to go where they don't want to go, or to do what they won't do. So long as you give in and express no preferences they will at their own pace take you anywhere they fancy. I soon understood the situation and merely sat, and assented. I never once used the reins as a means of propulsion, only as a means of balance.

Owing to the great heat inland and in observance of the rules of French-and-English we travelled by night, and slept, after a

fashion, by day. It is difficult for me now to say where exactly we
went, beyond indicating a south-easterly direction towards Monte
Cinto. The route was deliberately devious in order to bring us to
the dwellings of Dominique's relations and friends while avoiding
those of the Bonelli. For hours my mule followed his, slowly
picking its way over boulders up and down deep 'rias', and hover-
ing on precipitous tracks between the stars and waterless 'torrenti'.
We traversed forests of cork oak, chestnut and young pine. We
emerged upon plains of myrtle, arbutus, gum cistus and wild laven-
der. No wonder Corsica has been called 'the scented isle'. At night
the exotic smells of Mediterranean scrub and herb are always more
pungent than by day. In Corsica they are more intoxicating than
anywhere else. Dominique was the wayfarer's ideal guide. He was
infinitely resourceful and attentive; confident and alert. He spoke
little unless pressed and when on safe territory would sing the most
melancholy and blood-curdling ballads, verse after verse, which he
had learned by ear in infancy.

The days were not so relaxed. We would arrive before dawn at
what might look like a large heap of stones beside a solitary sentinel
cypress. This would be the residence of 'my sister-in-law's first
cousin and his wife, and her old mother.' Dominique would be
greeted with effusive embraces and cries of astonishment and pleasure. I would thereupon be introduced as his best friend and
patron, a Gothic lord from the foggy north, a sort of noble savage.
This was always flattering. No indecent curiosity was ever displayed in the presence of this outlandish visitor who was invariably
treated with touching hospitality, for which it was out of the question to offer payment. Indeed I was often embarrassed by it. These
poor peasants – for none showed signs of affluence from loot – who
toiled to scratch the barest necessities out of a barren soil would
produce breakfast of polenta and goat's cheese and a cask of sour
wine. They would watch the consumption of every mouthful,
exhorting me to eat and drink what I could with difficulty bring
myself to swallow. Worse still I would be offered the greatest of all
privileges which could not be declined, the host and hostess's bed,

usually a box of straw, or a mattress of sacking stuffed with hair and feathers. While the sun climbed into the burning sky I endeavoured to sleep. The flies alighted on exposed skin, the straw tickled, the feathers stifled, and invisible insects penetrated those parts of the anatomy that were covered. Dominique would throw himself down like a dog on a mat, if there was one, which he had carefully arranged in front of the door, and with his knife grasped firmly in one hand, or even in his teeth, sleep soundly, apparently impervious to flies and, unlike me, not incommoded by straw or insects.

Thus semi-refreshed we rose, dined – again on polenta, cheese and sour wine – and proceeded by moon or starlight. Wherever we went Dominique's password got us entry. At every stopping place mysterious messages as to the chief bandit's whereabouts were dispatched hither and thither, and delivered to us. The further we got into the mountains and the nearer to Spada's stronghold the more mysterious the directions became. Fresh arrow signs made with a stick in the dust, fresh notches on trees, or an odd angle at which a peasant woman adjusted a jug of water on her head at a well were often substitutes for the spoken word. It was tremendously exciting. I guessed that Spada, for ever on the run, seldom dared to spend more than one night in the same place. At last after a week's travelling we arrived at dawn before the mouth of a cave, over which trails of ivy hung in a green curtain. Outside the cave an old hag was indifferently stirring a metal pot suspended over a pile of blazing rosemary roots. Without looking up she nodded to Dominique who dismounted. He threw his mule's reins to me, saying 'Be prepared!' Then he walked deferentially into the cave. While waiting outside I was beside myself with anticipation. This was just the very setting I had imagined for a bandit chieftain. An eerie on a mountain slope inaccessible except to the initiated and the eagles from the beetling cliffs on either side. And behind this black cavity, room after room encrusted with pillaged treasure, where on leopard skins beneath twinkling oil lamps Aladdin himself, wearing a Byronic turban over flowing tresses, a braided velvet waistcoat, silk blouse fastened below the open neck with a garnet broach, and Turkish trousers, and puffing at a hookah, reclined among his myrmidons and concubines. My imagination was running away with me when Dominique reappeared, grinning with satisfaction. 'En ce moment le Maître est dans sa maison de campagne. The master has decided to receive you in proper style,' he said, jubilantly. 'Tomorrow,' he added.

This was a disappointment. 'Not in this heavenly cave?' I asked. 'Certainly not,' Dominique protested. 'He will receive you in his country house, where he seldom goes. You are greatly honoured.'

I forget where we slept that day. It was not in the cave, into which I was not permitted to set foot. I have always regretted that I did not insist upon it. I think we again lodged in some old cabin belonging to the uncle of a deceased second cousin once removed. The next night we left the mountains for the plains, and had a long downward trek. Midday brought us to a little provincial town on the main Bastia to Ajaccio road, along which motor lorries were trundling and raising dust. The suburb which we reached was very unpicturesque. We tied our mules to the gate of a modern detached villa standing, with others, in waste ground littered with discarded rubber tyres and tins. The house was labelled *Toi et Moi*. It had a front door within a Moorish arch. A terracotta dragon leant perilously over a gable encrusted with shiny yellow mosaics. Behind the thickly meshed curtains of the downstair windows small cactuses drooped in electro-plated pots. Dominique had been unusually silent all morning, declining to explain why we had left the maquis for this dismal locality, which was no different from a thousand other provincial suburbs in the *midi*.

We walked up a path of concrete crazy paving. Dominique boldly rang the bell. A genteel peroxide blonde opened the door. She ushered us through a passage which smelled of lentil soup into the equivalent of an English 'lounge', which smelled of cheese. Perched on the edge of a cheap settee was a mousey little man whom I took to be a commercial traveller off duty. He was dressed in pin-striped trousers and an off-the-peg, ill-fitting black jacket. He wore a celluloid dickie shirt front, collar and bow tie attached.

'Mon mari,' the peroxide blonde indicated. The commercial traveller rose and twitched a dapper little black moustache. He shook Dominique's forefinger, then mine. 'M'sieur Duval,' he muttered by way of self-introduction, motioning me to a steel chair and Dominique to a leather-covered pouf. He sat down again. On the jazzy wallpaper behind him a flight of china swallows rose diagonally from chair to picture rail. There were no pictures.

Madame Duval fetched an electroplated tray on which were a bottle with a wooden stopper carved in the likeness of Yvonne Printemps, and four glass thimbles, each bearing a transfer of Mickey Mouse. Into each thimble she poured a sticky liquid. Having politely raised them by way of further salutation the four of us sipped delicately and deposited the thimbles on paper doilies. There then ensued one of those irrefragable silences which sometimes overtake the highest circles of society. I looked at Dominique for a lead. He uttered not a word. Madame Duval offered us each a tiny, dry 'sablé'. 'Bon appetit!' murmured Monsieur Duval. We relapsed into even deeper silence. 'You live here all the year round?' I asked Madame Duval fatuously. 'Plaît-il?' said Monsieur Duval. The electroplated clock on the mantlepiece chimed a carillon from the Merry Peasant, twelve resonant strokes, and two shrill pings. Dominique seemed spellbound. But then I knew he was unaccustomed to being inside houses. Why, I asked myself, had he brought me to this one, in which I felt no more at ease then he looked? I had nothing to say to Monsieur Duval. Dominique clearly would not say anything to him. He merely stared at him with his mouth wide open. Was Monsieur Duval his *oncle à l'heritage* to whom he felt obliged to pay his respects from time to time in this taciturn fashion? Was I being exhibited as a sort of social stalking horse to show this middle-class couple what respectable company their nephew kept? If so, I was nonplussed how to show my paces without letting Dominique down. Whatever happened nothing would induce me to sleep in this hideous and pretentious villa. Give me his peasant relations' cabins, straw and bugs, any day, I decided. After the next carillon had struck and died away I rose. I gave Dominique a severe look. 'We must go,' I said. 'Good-bye, Madame Duval. Good-bye, Monsieur Duval.' It had been a ghastly and pointless visit. I was also very tired and our daily sleep was long overdue.

Once we had remounted our mules and were heading again for the maquis and the mountains Dominique turned upon me a face of transcendental rapture. 'Quelle finesse! Comme il est chevalier accompli! N'est ce pas qu'il est gentleman?' he exclaimed. 'Yes Dominique. Yes, of course,' I said. 'I do hope your uncle eventually leaves you a lot of money.' He looked rather baffled by this remark. I went on: 'Now we simply must get a little sleep somewhere before we are in a fit state to meet le Maître.' For a moment he looked more baffled still. Then he flushed darkly, and turning a pair of blazing eyes upon me, shouted, 'But you have just met him, you damned fool!' 'What! That little –' but I checked myself in time. 'Didn't I explain,' Dominique raged, 'that le Maître would receive us at his country house? An honour that he has never granted to anyone before! Who else did you suppose Monsieur Duval to be?' Sensibly I refrained from answering that question.

The return journey to Calvi was a slight anti-climax. If only Dominique had not been so absurdly mysterious. Had he only explained before ringing the bell at *Toi et Moi* just who Monsieur Duval was I would have known what to talk to him about. Or would that have been unwise in the peculiar circumstances? At least I could have studied him with the attention which that remarkable alibi deserved.

On leaving Corsica I took a boat from Bastia to Spezia to stay with the Lloyds in an isolated villa which they had rented from the Percy Lubbocks near Lerici. My disillusion with the ferocious Spada was not so absolute that I did not still identify myself with the Corsican bandits. I could think of little else, and my recent experiences were magnified into feats of dare-devilry that were scarcely justified. Moreover I arrived at the Lloyds' respectable house-party dressed in my bandit outfit, that is to say in a 'costume de chasse en velours bleu.' Round my waist I wore a wide scarlet sash with tasselled fringe, and attached to it the sheathed knife which Dominique had pressed upon me at parting in return for money to buy himself the revolver. I squirm with embarrassment whenever I recall the contemptuous smirk on the face of Professor Lindemann, who was one of the guests. His upper lip was contracted into his nostrils as though they were repulsing a revolting stench from a sewer. I quickly realized that I was making an ass of myself, and conformed to the clothing expected of a private secretary in 1933 even on the Mediterranean. But I never got to like the Prof as he was called. He was a frigid, calculating cynic, a disbeliever in and debunker of everything but scientific statistic. He also delighted in discomfiting simple people like myself in front of others. He overheard me describing to Lady Lloyd a seemingly innocuous dream I had just had. 'If you knew what you were saying,' he interrupted, 'you would desist. My interpretation of it is greatly to your discredit.' He needed no persuasion to give it to me when we were alone. 'But,' I pleaded, 'I have never, never had such inclinations as you are imputing to me.' 'You may not be aware of them,' this sinister man muttered in my ear. When I confided in Victor Cazalet, another guest, what Lindemann had just told me, he said: 'Don't worry. The Prof only means to implant ideas in one's head in order to denounce them. He gave a similar interpretation to one of my dreams a year ago.' 'What? Monkeys?' I asked. 'No. Ducks.' 'Worse and worse,' I said.

In the spring of 1934 I became a Catholic. I was twenty-five. Why at an age past sentimental adolescence, and one of full-blown, earthy youth, did I do it? Not for pietistic, but for temperamental reasons. I was a Christian. I did not feel that I belonged exclusively to the Church of England nor, as my father did, that God was an Englishman. So why not? I did not like to be called a convert. I saw myself as a re-vert to the ancient faith of my forebears. The Church of Rome was the original Christian church which for nearly two thousand years had survived countless heresies and schisms. I revered its endurance and its historic continuity which seemed to me divine. I admired the unbroken apostolic succession from St

Peter down to Pope Pius XI. I dearly loved the heraldry and symbolism of its ministry. I loved the Gothic sanctity, the Renaissance paganism, the Baroque opulence of the Catholic ritual and ceremonial. The smell of vellum missals, candle wax, chrism and incense was the breath of life to me. Genuflexions and signs of the Cross seemed the natural pledges of devotion, just as Gregorian chants and the *missa cantata* were the fitting stimulants and accompaniments to worship. I bitterly deplore the policy of the hierarchy today in depreciating and doing away with these time-honoured usages and practices.

I also think – in producing reasons for my reversion I could go on for ever, but will not – that I had need of a discipline from outside, a discipline with which unaided I was incapable of providing myself. Conscience was certainly not enough. Since no man's conscience agrees with another's why should mine be infallible? Of course I found much Catholic doctrine unpalatable. Several tenets seemed to me then, and still do seem, nonsensical. Very well, I ignore or flout them at my peril. But because they seem nonsensical I am not so arrogant as to presume they must be wrong. They may, for all I know, be useful yardsticks of ethical conduct. Besides, I believe in having pricks to kick against so long as one cannot kick them quite away. In the same sense I believe in outward proprieties. I don't care a fig what people do in private. In any case they all do it. I just don't want to see them do it, because 'it' is usually unaesthetic. There is much to be said for dissimulation as opposed to cant. For whereas the last clogs the wheels of daily intercourse the first often oils them.

On the whole then I found little hardship in accepting the Catholic dogmas. I have never, for instance, worried over the literal meaning of obscure passages in the Missal. Again it is the symbolism of the phraseology, tried and proved by countless assaults, and the poetry of the Latin words, weathered with the lichen and patina of the centuries, which are the ultimate beauties worth dying for. The reformers are mad – or wicked – to tamper with a foundation sanctified and beautified by the devout past, and to substitute makeshift structures of gimcrack materials merely in order to placate the ephemeral tastes of the vulgar and ignorant. By chucking overboard the Latin Mass these philistines are threatening the basic fabric of the Church's universality – an alarming and terrible thing to do.

My reversion to Catholicism had also a political connotation. I saw the Church as the last and impregnable bulwark against Communism in western Europe. The sequence of events in Spain throughout the Thirties confirmed my faith. If I had been more courageous physically and independent financially I would have fought for Franco when the civil war broke out. That I did not do so has been a lasting regret.

My father however saw my apostasy as he called it in quite a different light. He professed to be deeply shocked. He told my mother that she must expect me whenever the National Anthem was played to sit down, and put my hat on. To his friends he exclaimed in bewilderment. 'Whatever have I done to deserve this?' And to me on the only occasion when the matter was broached between us, 'It would not have been so mortifying if our church here had not been in the garden.' Considering how seldom he now attended it – for dear, long-suffering Canon Allsebrook was practically in his dotage and no longer a foe worth provoking – the objection was a non-sequitur. For a year or so afterwards I was not welcomed at home. Instead I often stayed for weekends at Broadway with Madame de Navarro who was my staunch supporter. From her house I could meet my mother on neutral ground. My father considered this behaviour gross disloyalty and, because Broadway was a mere three miles from where he lived, the addition of insult to injury.

Lord Lloyd was very sympathetic; and tolerant of my reversion. I think he was even a trifle envious. Being a strongly entrenched Anglo-Catholic he wondered how a Protestant could go quite so far. 'Can you really swallow the Pope?' he asked. 'Hook, line and sinker,' I replied.

By 1935 it became apparent that I ought to have a permanent job which offered what are called prospects. I could not live indefinitely on a private secretary's salary, agreeable though my actual occupation was. I must earn more money. Lord Lloyd with the kindest intentions got me into Reuters. I left him with heartfelt gratitude and regret.

From the very start I knew that Reuters was not my, and I was not going to be its, cup of tea. My dreamy temperament was hopelessly unsuited to the slick purpose of news scooping. I was far too slow and totally lacking push. Besides, I was absolutely indifferent whether Reuters or the Press Association were first to learn and pass on to the *Daily Sketch* that Swaziland was about to invade Mozambique, or that King Zog was engaged to the daughter of a greengrocer. Neither mattered to me in the very least. Yet it was necessary to suppose it did if one wished to be a success in this distributary of daily incident and sensation.

Because of my recent employment I was made third and junior secretary to the chairman, Sir Roderick Jones. The appointment was looked upon as a firm rung on the Reuters ladder, albeit the bottom rung of all. Unfortunately Sir Roderick and I were in all respects antipodal. There is no need to expatiate further upon my deficiencies with which by now the reader is all too familiar. Let me then concentrate for a moment on Sir Roderick's. He was in stature a little undersized. He was spruce, and dapper, and perky. I would describe his appearance as that of a sparrow were it not for his waist which, instead of being loose, was tight, pinched in by a conspicuous double-breasted waistcoat which he habitually wore like a corset. This constrictive garment gave him the shape of a magnified wasp. His face too resembled that of a wasp seen under a microscope. It was long and the bulbous nose was proboscis-like. His small eyes darted rapidly in his head in the manner of that insect. They never rested on their victim, yet because of a feverish activity missed nothing. His mouth too was sharp and vespine. His sting was formidable and unlike the bee's could be repeated.

Sir Roderick Jones was intensely proud of the exalted position he occupied in Fleet Street and the world of power. He wished his influence to be felt by the great and humble, particularly the humble. When his Rolls Royce drove up each morning to the main entrance of Reuters a bell rang violently in every room and passage of the building to announce the chairman's arrival. There was a general scurry and flurry of alarm. When it drove off in the evening another bell rang more softly. There was a contrasting sigh of relief and relaxation of tension.

I have no doubt that Sir Roderick was a loving and loved husband and father. As an employer he was not likeable. He was the very reincarnation of Martinet, without the grisly charm of that French drill-master. He devised an office routine from which no deviation was permissible in any circumstance. He demanded from his underlings the strictest observance of infinitesimal minutiae. For instance, every object on his desk had to be arranged each morning with meticulous exactitude. The edges of the in-tray must be flush with those of the out-tray. The silver calendar, turned for the day, two inches to the left of the clock. Pencils newly sharpened, and clean nibs in pen-holders. The penwiper at right angles to the blotter, freshly filled. Telephones and intercommunicator slightly staggered at an angle of, say, 22½ degrees from the chair. Envelope rack within easy reach without necessitating undue stretching, yet not so close that the elbow had to be unnaturally crooked. If the softest of the three india rubbers was not found on the left-hand side of the row on the allotted tray and adjacent to the red (not blue) sealing-wax, Sir Roderick's displeasure could be terrible.

As third secretary I was responsible for the daily arrangement of Sir Roderick's desk. I also took down and typed out the less important letters he cared to dictate to me. If he detected that a single word had been rubbed out and retyped, the whole page, complete with four carbon copies, was sent back to be done again no matter how late in the evening it was. I was only allowed to draft letters to shops. I once worded a letter to Trumpers as follows: 'Dear Sirs, Will you kindly send me a medium-sized bottle (no. 2) of your "Ecstatic" brilliantine, Yours faithfully (Sgd) Roderick Jones, K.B.E., Chairman and Managing Director of Reuters.' Sir

Roderick returned unsigned the typed draft with a pencil line through it and the querulous comment, 'Kindly send is not grammar.' I retyped and submitted a second draft: 'Dear Sirs, Will you send me kindly a medium-sized bottle, etc.' This draft was likewise returned scratched out, with a caustic note, 'Are you trying to be funny, Mr Milne?' Sir Roderick's abbreviation of my surname always nettled me, as it was intended to do. I submitted a third draft: 'Dear Sirs, Will kindly you send me a medium-sized bottle . . . ' Again the sheet was returned, this time torn in half with an angry pencil scrawl, 'You are clearly being insubordinate.' For the fourth time I typed, in capital letters, these words: 'SIRS, SEND ME A SPECIMEN OF YOUR NUMBER 2.' I fired this impertinent missive into Sir Roderick's room and stalked out of the building. Next morning I turned up at Reuters in some trepidation. To my amazement not a word was said by Sir Roderick on the subject.

Often I was kept in the office till 8.30 for perfectly frivolous reasons, such as typing out his children's poetry, to be sent round by special messenger to his London house for the edification of his guests at a dinner party. At eight o'clock he might telephone through to suggest an improvement in the scansion, or direct me to Boots in Piccadilly (open all night), to buy and deliver myself by breakfast time next morning a jar of Cod Liver Oil.

On red letter days I would be dispatched to present with Sir Roderick's compliments an enormous bouquet of exotic flowers to Lady So-and-So or the Duchess of This-and-That on the Golden Arrow platform of Victoria station. The departing ladies were always beautiful and sophisticated. I enjoyed these commissions and it was fun trying to guess how much the object of Sir Roderick's attentions reciprocated them. The majority were, I think, more flattered than touched. They were invariably charming and grateful to me just as though I had paid for the expensive flowers. One actually gave me a kiss in the carriage. I rejoiced to think how cross Sir Roderick would be if he knew.

I enjoyed less the luncheon parties he laid on for the editors of foreign and imperial newspapers at the Savoy Hotel. I was not invited to them of course. Instead I was warned the evening before to put on my best suit and above all Old Etonian tie – an important detail – and be in attendance at the restaurant next day. My duty was to show the guests the way to the lavatory and hold out a towel to the most distinguished – they all looked to me alike – as they washed their hands. I would thereupon hold out my hand (I was strictly enjoined not to do this) and sometimes collected several pounds this way. I learned that one should always let the next man see what his predecessor was giving, for tips are as much the fruit of blackmail as of a generous disposition.

Nevertheless I was extremely unhappy at Reuters. It was, with the exception of the War, the most down of all my down periods. It was made worse by an emotional predicament (I wanted to get married) and the realization that I was being a failure in a job from which the right sort of man would have profited. I was clearly the wrong sort of man. There was no doubt about it whatever. My obvious unsuitability would, I knew, shortly provoke a crisis. Sure enough it came one Friday evening.

Sir Roderick was waiting for the Rolls to take him to Sussex for the weekend. It was incumbent upon me to warn him the moment it arrived. The hall porter rang to tell me the chauffeur was at the door. I forgot to inform Sir Roderick, who was pacing up and down his room watch in hand. Happening to pass the window he looked out and saw the Rolls and the chauffeur, with rug over one arm, standing patiently beside it. He called me into the room. Angrily he demanded why I had not told him. He had already lost five precious minutes which the Empire could ill spare. Was I deliberately obstructive? Or was I merely a fool? He could not decide which. Neither could I. I only knew what he knew, that it was quite unnecessary for him to be told, because neither the Rolls nor he was ever one split second behind the pre-ordained time.

Sir Roderick worked himself into a towering rage. The slanting sun was pouring into the room. He had his back to it, looking no longer like a magnified wasp but a plethoric turkey cock. Very unprepossessing he was too. But the fine particles of his spit caught in the evening sunlight made a fanlike spray which issued with the velocity and subsided on to the pile carpet with the delicacy of the great Apollo Fountain at Versailles. Though the display was in miniature it was no less remarkable than the beautiful prototype of Le Nôtre's contriving. I was so fascinated by this performance which was being repeated for my benefit with each torrent of invective that I paid no heed to what Sir Roderick was saying, and stood blandly smiling. A cloud passed over the sun, the Apollo Fountain was switched off, and I heard the turkey cock splutter, 'Well, I can't stop to argue about it any further now, Mr Milne. We will discuss the matter again on Monday.'

It was thus rudely brought to my intelligence that on Monday I would most probably be given the sack. This would certainly not do. It would be like being sent down from Eton without one's leaving book. I would never be able to get another job. My father would be triumphant. Lord Lloyd would be distressed. Every friend would be deceived in me. Besides, I would starve. What was I to do? I racked my brain all that night to no avail. Sooner than I could have hoped for advice came from an unexpected quarter – conveniently enough, from the Prime Minister.

I had been invited to spend that Saturday to Monday, as a weekend was then termed, by Lord and Lady FitzAlan at Cumberland Lodge in Windsor Park. Lord FitzAlan belonged to a now totally vanished age and species. He was an extremely patrician and saintly old man, whom it was impossible not to revere and love. During the years of his nephew the Duke of Norfolk's minority he had been the first Catholic layman in this country. He still played a leading rôle in Catholic affairs. His advice was sought and heeded over church policy and appointments, including the election of successive Archbishops of Westminster and even the conferring of cardinals' hats. As an elder statesman in the House of Lords he was likewise mentor to many Conservative peers. Lord Lloyd, through whom I got to know him, greatly valued his sage counsel.

Both FitzAlans were by their nature protective and hospitable. I often stayed with and became devoted to them. For all their wisdom and broadmindedness they did not belong to the 20th century. They had their roots firmly in the Victorian age and were like two precious conservatory vines which, first planted in the 1850s, still continued to put forth fruit in a less sheltered age and climate. In actual appearance he with his stocky figure and drooping moustache resembled the walrus, and she with her sharp, tormented features the carpenter in *Alice Through the Looking-Glass*.

This particular weekend – for I must relapse into the current vernacular – represents to me the last posthumous fling of the polite nineties. The house-party of fourteen consisted, with the exception of the FitzAlans' unmarried daughter Magdalen (a sad and docile woman of my father's age) and myself, of people whose mature youth had coincided with that decade. They were Lord and Lady Salisbury (he had been an under-secretary of state in Queen Victoria's reign), General Sir John and Lady Isobel Gathorne-Hardy (he was a Boer War veteran), Sir David Hunter Blair, Abbot of Fort Augustus (he became a Benedictine monk in the Seventies), Lady Abingdon (who was my friend Johnnie Churchill's grandmother), Sir Edward Marsh, Mrs Belloc Lowndes, and Mr and Mrs Stanley Baldwin. The two with whom I made instant friends were Eddie Marsh and Marie Belloc Lowndes. Eddie and I were put in the bachelor wing of this stark and gloomy house. I have a recollection of the prim and virginal man of letters sitting, after we had all retired on Saturday night, bolt upright on the end of my bed, half undressed in a collarless starched shirt and a pair of thick cotton combinations down to the ankles. While he recited interminable passages from *Paradise Lost* I was transfixed by the brass stud which bobbed up and down his Adam's apple until I fell fast asleep. I think I forfeited his esteem from that moment. Mrs Belloc Lowndes on the other hand was often to invite me to dine alone in her snug little house in Barton Street. She loved intimacy and gossip. I had been cautioned that she wormed her way into people's confidences; that they thought they were clutching a plump little dove to their bosoms until they found out that it was an asp. I had no such experience. I was however enchanted by her shameless greed. On arrival at her house she would pour into my glass from a large jug brimful of what looked like lemonade, a potent white lady cocktail. Having done this she would toss the remaining contents of the jug down her own throat in one gulp. It had absolutely no ill effects upon her; and in no case was she what is called intemperate where drink was concerned. One exceedingly hot day in mid-summer I gave her luncheon at Wilton's oyster bar. Together we stuffed ourselves with oysters and lobsters, accompanied by a heap of brown bread and butter, washed down with stout. We finished with cheese and port. When the ruinously expensive meal was over I piloted Mrs Belloc Lowndes across the sanded floor – it was like rolling an enormous puff ball along the beach – into the street. She was puce in the face, replete and contented. Our tête-à-tête had been an unqualified success. I hailed a cab and after an affectionate hug pushed her inside. 'Where shall I tell the driver to go to?' I asked. 'Oh, I'll direct him,' she said as she waved me good-bye. I saw her lean from the seat to the glass partition, and overheard her direction to the driver, 'Take me straight to Gunters, please.'

An interesting commentary upon the Cumberland Lodge visit is the amount of changing of clothes that took place. Not one of the guests was chic, or fashionable. Not one of them, I am sure, took the least interest in what he or she wore. Certainly no single garment among the fourteen of us, except one of Mrs Baldwin's hats, a confection of tulle snow and seven birds of paradise, is mem-orable. Yet the changing was incessant. We (and here I should exclude myself lest it be thought I boast, for my wardrobe was then strictly limited) first assembled in breakfast clothes at 9 o'clock. We changed for church at 11. We changed for luncheon at 1.30. Those of us who went for an afternoon stroll in Windsor Park changed at 3. We certainly changed for tea at 5. Thereafter I do not think we changed again until the dressing gong went at 8. Then we changed to some tune, the women into long trailing gowns, and the men into tails and white ties. Some of us therefore put on six different gar-ments that day as a matter of custom, not vanity.

In June of this year Mr Baldwin had become Prime Minister for the third time. He was the FitzAlans' most honoured guest. Everyone deferred to him and sought to engage him in conversation. I purposely kept out of his way and the first day he did not address a word to me. I did not expect him to. He seemed preoccupied and dreadfully gruff, hardly responding to Mrs Baldwin who was being extremely jolly with everyone and determined to keep the ball rolling. She completely won my heart by her naturalness and unpremeditated remarks which were shrewd as well as amusing. At dinner she teased us all and was the star turn. Mr Baldwin sat in stolid silence until dessert when he selected a Worcester Permaine apple and without peeling it with the silver knife provided, chewed it and spat the pips into his plate. When the port came round he produced his pipe and pouch from a deep pocket – a volume of Lucretius came out with them – and lit up. For the rest of the evening he was jovial, almost bantering, but not yet charming.

The next morning I woke with a start. A figure was moving at the foot of the bed. At first I thought it must still be Eddie Marsh. Had he got to the end of *Paradise Lost*? And had he noticed that I had dozed off? No, it was the footman folding my evening clothes. 'There is a note, sir, with your tea,' he said. Bleary-eyed I read, 'J.L-M. If you are doing nothing better, come for a walk before breakfast. Leaving 7.45. S.B.' Heavens, it was 7.30 already! 'Yes,' I shouted to the footman. 'Tell him yes,' and I jumped out of bed. I was astonished, and thrilled to the marrow.

Mr Baldwin was in the hall, pipe in mouth and stick in hand. The scuttling under-housemaids seemed put out by the unwonted descent of two house guests at this unseasonable hour when the front rooms were their recognized province. We hardly disturbed them, and let ourselves out into the garden. 'I thought it would be rather fun to have a talk by ourselves about old times,' he said. As we crossed the dewy lawn a bowler hat shot up from a rhododendron bush on our right. A few further paces and a second bowler hat emerged from the Portuguese laurel on our left. Mr Baldwin paid not the slightest attention. The bowler hats let us pass through a little iron gate that led into the Park and converged behind us. Out of the corner of one eye I had a glance of two horribly inscrutable faces with square jowls, and two pairs of holstered hips. I was alarmed. Were they going to assassinate the Prime Minister? And ought I to alert him? Casually so as not to create panic I mentioned what I had seen. 'Drat them!' said Mr Baldwin. 'Tweedledum and Tweedledee. Yes, I suppose they are there.' He did not trouble to look round. I realized that I had been mistaken. For an hour and a half they shadowed us persistently except once when my companion, with infinite cunning in doubling back on his tracks in a wood, managed to throw them off the scent. This successful feint amused him vastly, although he did not allude to them nor once turn his head in their direction.

The 'old times' were very old times indeed, and referred to places and mutual friends of the Baldwins and my grandparents in the Bewdley neighbourhood before the First War. He recalled the croquet tournaments at my grandmother's house and my mother's astounding prowess at the game. Did she still play? No, and I was quite unaware that anyone so impatient could ever have done such a thing. (The next time I saw my mother I passed on this meed of praise. Her comment was, 'So long as skirts were worn to the ground you have no idea how successful I was. Cheating the Baldwins was as easy as falling off a log.') Did I remember these parties? Yes I did, and the occasion when for some misdemeanour I was locked into a little room at the top of one of the towers and in a rage scattered from the window to the croquet lawn below several packets of lavatory paper which were stored there. My grandmother was scandalized not by my protest, but the manner of it. She predicted that a child who could think up so indelicate a means of drawing attention to himself must come to a sticky end. Mr Baldwin made no reference to this incident which very possibly had escaped his memory, although at the time it can hardly have escaped his notice.

His love of Worcestershire, that 'wonderfully dim county' in the opinion of John Betjeman, was touching. He was part of it; and it was part of him. Indeed he resembled it, by which I mean its physical contours on the map. For he was rugged, jagged and unspectacular. Yet like the Worcestershire of my youth still natural, incorruptible and jealously preserving depths of poetry and beauty, which had to be looked for to be appreciated. During our walk he spoke with feeling about Mary Webb who had captured the spirit of the West Midlands people, and died without the recognition she deserved. He said, 'If I have helped towards establishing her posthumous fame I have achieved something,' a remark which struck me as the quintessence of humility. From that moment he had much charm for me.

'And now about yourself?' Mr Baldwin asked as he sidestepped unexpectedly into a concealed path which led off the ride we had been smartly pacing down. He dragged me after him behind a tree. The bowler hats, grunting and grumbling, passed unobserving within a few feet of us in straight pursuit of what was not. 'Lord FitzAlan mentioned that you are now working at Reuters.' I told him I was junior secretary to Sir Roderick Jones. 'That's grave,' said Mr Baldwin. Encouraged by the pejorative tone of his word 'grave' and the sudden warmth of his manner I poured out everything, how bad I was at my job, how much I hated it, how entirely dependent on it I was, and that tomorrow I was almost certainly going to be sacked. Before I had finished I thought how intolerable it was to bore with my paltry woes the Prime Minister of Great Britain who at this time was wrestling with every conceivable issue of national and international importance. Who was I, practically unknown to him, to spoil his one morning's relaxation in the week from the cares of his onerous office? I felt very ashamed. I need not have been. He expressed a most fatherly concern and was extremely sympathetic.

He stopped abruptly to bang his stick on the ground. The two bowler hats, who were hot on our heels again, practically knocked us down. Mr Baldwin reflected. 'What you must do,' he said with emphasis, 'is this. You must get your notice in first. Immediately, without delay. Tomorrow morning. This will take the wind out of his sails. Having done so you must not repine. Friends will come to your rescue. Do not have silly scruples about accepting help and money which you cannot repay. At your age you are bound to get a job you like eventually, doubtless sooner than you expect. Remember that lean times never last for ever.' This was simple, straightforward stuff, hackneyed if you like. How I treasured and acted upon his advice. I never met Mr Baldwin again. But I have loved him ever since.

Next morning I left a note on Sir Roderick Jones's writing-table asking for an interview as soon as possible. 'Yes, you certainly may see me now,' he shouted down the intercommunicator in a menacing fashion soon after he reached the office. I went into his room. What I knew to be my last vision of him – *in cathedra* so to speak, because for years afterwards I used to see him in my club, where we never spoke to one another – did not alarm me. It strengthened my resolve. 'Well, Mr Milne,' he began, 'there is something further I have to say to you.' He paused, licking his chops – there is no other term for it. 'There is something I have to say to you first, Sir Roderick,' I broke in rather offensively. 'I know I was to blame for not telling you on Friday what of course you knew already, namely that your Rolls Royce had arrived. I merely forgot. I'm sorry. But I am not sorry to tell you how much, how extremely much I have disliked working for you. I wish to give you notice. I am leaving now.'

'Oh, are you indeed? And who, I would like to know, has advised you to do this foolish thing?' he said with a sneer.

'The Prime Minister, Sir Roderick,' I answered swelling with self-satisfaction. 'And if you don't believe me, you can ask him. Good-bye!' I turned and left him, and Reuters, for good and all.

I daresay I lacked discretion and taste in bringing Mr Baldwin's name into this altercation. I just could not resist it. I guessed Sir Roderick was unlikely to check the truth of what I had said. I knew too that he knew it to be the truth.

VIII

MARS ULTOR

MR BALDWIN was absolutely right. Friends did come to the rescue. They offered me hospitality and money, both of which I accepted with alacrity, bearing firmly in mind that charity grows stale as soon as it is taken for granted. Women are naturally more sympathetic to men in distress than men are and I daresay, although I am not certain, that the inverse rule applies to our sex. In all cases women are far more understanding and generous. They are also more loyal and more practical.

Again I stayed with my kind old friend in Northamptonshire. She made it clear that I might come and go when I pleased. She put a room at my disposal and never once complained that I treated her in return like an unpaid hotel proprietor, nor asked how long the unsolicited visit might last. It lasted quite three months, with intermittent jaunts to London for which she supplied the cash. There I used to stay with Harold Nicolson who had rooms in King's Bench Walk, and looked for jobs. In the mid-thirties they were harder to come by than they are today. The world did not then feel under obligation to support unqualified youth. Nor was unqualified youth organized to protest against this unfair neglect of its unproven talents by marching, smashing telephone kiosks, stubbing cigarette ends into police horses' rumps, sitting-in, lying-in, renouncing soap and water, stinking to high heaven and looking like gorillas. On the contrary it suffered in dismal silence while trying to keep up an appearance of well-being, without which it would never have been offered the most menial task. For in those pre-hygienic days even a garbage man (to use an archaic term for a refuse disposal officer) was expected to look, and smell, like a human being.

The old adage that beggars can't be choosers was entirely disregarded by me. Once bitten twice shy seemed far more appropriate. I was determined not to go into business – if indeed a business had been so ill-advised as to invite me – nor to accept a job that offered adequate remuneration but nothing else. Suddenly the very job of which I had dreamt when at Oxford and did not believe existed, presented itself. The National Trust was launching a new scheme to save some of the historic houses of England, and needed a secretary. Vita Sackville West, whose memory I bless on this account as well as a hundred others, recommended me to the Trust. In March 1936 I began to work for this body with which, although no longer on its staff, I am still connected. Since the National Trust is almost the only living link with the other me now dead and buried, and belongs as much to the present as the past, it would be indecent to embalm any substance of it in this antiquated chronicle.

I will merely say that the three and a half years before the outbreak of the second World War were about the happiest, because most fulfilled of my life. The National Trust was then truly a vocation, not a profession. The male staff – it numbered four amateurs – received very low salaries. Mine was £400 a year on which, unsupplemented by any allowance or income of my own, I somehow managed to live. During those starry-eyed years my work was a dedication to building up an organization in which I passionately believed. Until 1939 there was still a last-hour chance of saving the agrarian landscape of the most beautiful country in northern Europe, if only the public and Parliament could be roused to insist upon far-reaching, imaginative planning. Alas, the chance passed by. Public and Parliament have proved largely indifferent, and our half-hearted efforts have been overtaken by unrestrained technological greed. Those parts of the country scene, other than national parks, which are not irredeemably ruined will, so rapid is the pace of 'progress', soon be so.

My devotion to the National Trust was nearly matched by my interest in the foundation of the Georgian Group. Its principal promoter was Robert Byron in whose little Chelsea house I lodged for much of this time. The Group's purpose which by the outbreak of the war it had fairly accomplished was not so much to save individual buildings – it was too poor and powerless for this – as to teach the public that Georgian architecture mattered. Until the late thirties it was not at all appreciated by local authorities or government departments (the Ministry of Works did not even acknowledge that a building of later date than 1714 could have merit). Today all is changed. Every borough engineer discourses learnedly on the comparative merits of houses by Adam and Wyatt, Soane and Nash. And the result of the new awareness of the Georgian townscape is most manifest – namely, the mutilation or destruction of practically every Georgian street and terrace in every city of the British Isles. The original members of the Georgian Group committee were all close friends with sophisticated tastes and fearless in their denunciation of philistinism. Robert Byron in a pamphlet referred to the Bishop of London, whom he held responsible for the demolition of Wren City churches, as 'that mitred serpent', and a well-known Countess prevented the disappearance of Abingdon Street, Westminster by threatening to chain herself and some sister peeresses to the area railings. The street was thereupon reprieved, only to be pulled down without a murmur of protest the moment the war was over.

Those years of intensive build-up of the National Trust properties and of Georgian Group nuisance value were overshadowed by world events. A terrible anxiety gnawed at the vitals. I felt in the pit of the stomach that same abysmal sickness from which I suffered as a child when a ghastly awareness of the first war gradually impressed itself upon my conscience. The inevitability of conflict brooded like an ever darkening cloud. Desperately, irrationally one hoped that, so unpredictable are storm clouds, it might providentially dissolve or drift away. But not being subject to the winds of chance which attend natural phenomena, this cloud had to burst over Europe. When war came there was something like panic in moving offices out of London. I helped cram the National Trust equipment into a pair of minute Lutyens pavilions on Runnymede meadows. Files, papers, typewriters and confusion unmentionable were left to be sorted by one ailing secretary and two stalwart, imperturbable ladies.

I straightway joined the Red Cross and was posted to a Civil Defence station in West Brompton. There was plenty of time for contemplation, twelve hours out of every twenty-four, either by day aimlessly wandering round an asphalt yard, or by night lying swathed in any army blanket on the concrete floor of a warehouse near the World's End. For six months I thus waited for the bombs to fall on London, and pondered. What ought I to do? The first war had made many of my generation pacifists. I still contend that those who were brave enough to be pacifists in 1914, and those who honestly saw the issues of 1939 to be the same as they were in the first war were not ignoble, however much the latter may have been mistaken. For the first war was not one between conflicting ideals, but of nations against nations. Such a war is inexcusable. A man should not consent at his Government's dictation to fight an enemy simply because he is a German or a Russian. It does not make sense to hate the whole German or Russian people. One can only hate people whom one knows, that is to say one's neighbours if they trespass upon one's home ground, or one's countrymen if they threaten to undermine the constitution of one's country. In other words the only valid excuse for fighting others is personal indignation. Therefore a civil war, terrible though it be, seems to me an understandable and possibly justifiable kind of war. For then one is obviously not fighting, if one be English, other people for being English, but one is fighting to repel some devilry which one believes to be threatening one's cherished way of life. Had I for instance fought for Franco I would have done so not in order to kill Spaniards, but to help Spaniards repel what they and I considered a diabolical creed threatening the European Christian ideal.

While during the phoney war I was wasting time with the Red

Cross I came to the conclusion that I should fight. I was much influenced by a letter from Robert Byron in answer to one I had written him about my perplexities. 'If you say you refuse to kill your fellow men; if you maintain that the evil caused by war out-weighs any good that war can preserve; if you are prepared to envisage the conditions of life that would result from our not fight-ing, and to accept such a prospect as preferable to war; and if you believe that by your personal pacifism you are contributing all you can to the avoidance of war in the future, then I will receive your opinions with respect and ask you to explain them further.' And he finished with this sentence; 'Whether one is a pacifist or not, one must admit that pacifism isn't going to get us out of the mess now we are in it. Therefore it seems to me that the only thing to do and the only way to comport oneself is to determine to clear up the mess afterwards and to carry the techniques of preventing war perhaps one, perhaps the whole stage further.'

My decisive motive for not remaining a pacifist was that at this time we were ostensibly fighting the two diabolical systems, Nazism and Communism, then in unholy alliance. Indeed until 1941 Russia was giving economic aid to Germany, and that very year Stalin and Hitler were planning a division of the British Empire between them. Could I have foreseen during the phoney war that in a year and a half's time the tables would have turned and we should be allied with Russian Bolshevism I might not have reached my conclusions quite so readily. For after June 1941 the war ceased to be a fight to maintain ideals, and became a war of nations against nations. The allies were determined to crush not merely Nazism, but Germany for the benefit, as things have turned out, of Bolshevism. This was brought about by our insistence upon Germany's unconditional surrender long after Nazism was doomed. The consequence of our compromise with Russian poli-cies needs no stressing – the hideous partition of Europe and the rising triumph of world Communism.

I must confess that I am not a brave man. I doubt, even if I had been convinced of the iniquity of fighting in 1939–40, whether I

could have summoned enough courage to carry through my pacifism to the end. It was easier and less frightening to do what the
majority of one's friends were doing, and accept whatever came to
one. My friends, I said to myself, were just as sensitive, just as
unbloodthirsty, and probably more honourable and honest than I.
How therefore could I sincerely set myself apart in comfort and
safety, and refuse to share with them the same ordeals? So in the
early spring of 1940 I enlisted. While waiting to be called up I organized an exhibition in Cheyne Walk of desultory works of art associated with Chelsea, almost anything that could be gathered
together at that time, in aid of the Finns whose country had been
cruelly invaded by Russia.

By midsummer I received my papers and joined the Irish
Guards' Training Battalion at Lingfield. Here I made a grievous
mistake. Because I was by temperament wholly unfitted for the
army and wholly devoid of that prized public school quality, lead-
ership, I should have joined the ranks, with a view to rising from
them in due course if I proved worthy of a commission. This I had
wanted to do, but allowed myself to be dissuaded. Being over thirty
I was able to bypass the rigours of a guardsman's life at Caterham,
and become an ensign immediately. By this time the phoney war
months of leisurely preparation were over. Terrible events had
already happened. The British Expeditionary Force had with-
drawn from Dunkirk in early June. France had fallen on the 17th of
the month. The dismal day is imprinted on my memory by an irrelevant incident. I was staying at West Wycombe Park. The large
house was filled to overflowing with evacuees of one sort and
another. All the servants had already left for war work except one
ancient family butler, Black. Our hostess was then estate agent,
housekeeper, cook, kitchenmaid, parlourmaid, housemaid and odd
woman combined. Rations were limited. We were fed on whatever
scraps the dwindling estate could muster. Struck dumb with
consternation and misery by the morning's news we sat at the luncheon table. Black pottered around the room, bent double with
rheumatism, his face the picture of customary woe. 'Will you have

swan or sucking pig, m'lady?' he asked our hostess without bog-
gling at the inapposite occasion for such a remark.

France had fallen. Great Britain stood alone. She was awaiting
the next assault. The Brigade of Guards had already suffered lamentable losses. In consequence my battalion could only spare the
minimum time for training raw officers. Like Lord Lloyd who in
1931 assumed that I was going to prove a good secretary, my battalion in this desperate summer of 1940 assumed that I would prove a
good officer. I regret that this assumption was not justified.

At once I felt at a great disadvantage with my co-ensigns who
unlike me had reached the rank after many months of arduous
training at Caterham. They knew the ropes. I did not. Their
extreme youth was as disconcerting as their prowess. The extreme
youth of my seniors in rank did not matter so much because these
full lieutenants and captains were of course expected to be versed
in the intricacies of regimental practice. I rather enjoyed being
coached in social etiquette by a wonderfully self-confident lieuten-
ant of 19. 'When you go to London,' he cautioned, 'don't say, "I'm
off to town." Whatever you do, never, never be seen carrying a
parcel, not even a tube of toothpaste.' 'What then should we do if
we find ourselves obliged to buy some toothpaste?' we asked in
bewilderment. 'You must have it sent,' said this young man who
had just returned from a week's participation in the carnage of
Calais, 'round to the Ritz, or wherever you may be staying. And one
more thing,' he went on. 'When someone greets you with "How
d'you do?" you must not reply, "I'm doing nicely, thanks."' 'Thank
you,' we said, 'for the hint. We won't.'

The Medical Officer's advice was likewise useful. 'You *must* wash
under the arms, you know,' he said fiercely. 'And after every
evacuation you must have a bath.' 'A bath every time?' one of us
asked. 'Even if I have what is euphemistically termed diarrhoea?' 'I
repeat, after *every* evacuation, a bath.' The Medical Officer was
emphatic. Only the Battalion Chaplain made allowances for the
human flesh. 'Don't think I don't know that boys will be boys. Of
course they will be. Don't think Our Blessed Lord wouldn't also

have been, if indeed he had been one, which of course he never was. At least not in the sense you mean, I mean. Anyway, boys, don't be boys too often, if you know what I mean. Got it?' He was a good man, brimful of the milk of human understanding.

It was agonizingly like being at school again where the other boys are more alarming than the masters. The bonhomie of mess life was particularly trying. As for the christian names, the army's use of them led to some awkward situations. When on the parade ground one had to report to the Colonel that Captain So-and-So's company was on the war path, one knew that officer only as Pat, being totally ignorant of his surname. One was thereupon obliged in a flash to invent Fitzmaurice or The O'Donoghue, whichever sounded the more Irish or probable, and hope one had struck lucky. By far my worst disability was chronic astigmatism and myopia combined. I would never have got a commission in the Brigade if I had worn spectacles. Indeed I needed two pairs, one for long, one for short sight. Without either I see everything in a delicious haze – delicious because until I put on my spectacles, objects, especially human objects, can look tantalizingly beautiful – and, even when screwing my eyeballs to pinpoints, nothing clearly. But the consequences were disastrous when drilling. I never saw when to give words of command.

It was only fairly easy to get a company moving. One shouted Attention, Slope Arms, Form Fours, Left Turn and Quick March! But it was incredibly difficult to get the brutes to stop. Guardsmen are so highly trained that when an officer gives a wrong word of command they are expected to pay no attention. Otherwise they get a severe wigging from the sergeant-major, that most alarming of all mortals. He stands on the parade ground between the officer and the company, his feet together, arms straight down his sides, stick under left arm, a rigid, poker apostrophe of efficiency and terror. When a wrong command is given and a few guardsmen obey, the sergeant-major screams at them, abuses them like pick-pockets while pretending that the officer did it on purpose in order to catch them out. No one of course, least of all the abused, is taken in by this face-saving device. Having cursed the guardsmen into heaps and brought them to attention again the sergeant-major turns briskly round, clicks his heels and salutes the officer, indicating that he may start afresh. In doing so he gives from under his peaked cap and over his bristling moustache a quick look of such contempt at and warning to the officer not to be a bloody fool a second, third, or fourth time, whichever it may be, that it is enough to strike him dead on the spot. The sergeant-major about-turns again, his back to the officer, and the world awaits a repetition of the miserable ensign's ignominy. After five or six of these mortifying experiences the humiliated ensign may get the company on the march. I have said that to do this is only fairly easy. There then ensues a brief moment for self-congratulation before the worse predicament arises – how to halt them. I shall return to this distressing theme very shortly.

I had spent barely a month at the training barracks at Lingfield, when I was posted to Dover. The Battle of Britain was in full swing. Hitler's invasion of England was expected at any moment. We lived on the alert. Day and night an officer was kept on duty awaiting from some higher intelligence the warning code signal, 'Oliver Cromwell'. When this ominous name came down the telephone the officer knew that the invasion was on the way. He must instantly without wasting a second ring through to the Colonel and arouse the whole battalion. At 3 o'clock one morning it was my turn to be on duty. Rather drowsily I was reading *Barchester Towers*. The telephone rang. I picked up the receiver. 'This is Higher Command QE2X speaking,' came from a rather cissy voice a long way off. 'I say, old boy, sorry to tell you – Oliver Cromwell!' 'What?' I screamed, my heart in my boots. 'Are you sure? Are you absolutely sure?' I had no reason for questioning the man's words beyond the utter horror of the announcement. 'Well, I may have got it wrong,' the voice said affectedly. 'Then for dear Christ's sake,' I pleaded, 'do get it right.' There was a pause, during which I had my finger on the special telephone to the Colonel's bedroom, as it were on the pulse of England. 'Sorry, old chap,' the voice came back again. 'It's only Wat Tyler. I get so confused with these historical blokes.' 'Wat Tyler,' I said sharply, 'was a very different sort of bloke indeed. He didn't unleash hell and damnation like the other. No doubt he would have liked to. But he was strung up by the Lord Mayor before he got a chance. You deserve no less for giving me the fright of my life. So good night to you, or good morning, or whatever it is!'

Our battalion was called blotting paper troops. We were told that when the Germans landed our task was to hold out for half an hour until the crack regiments a few miles inland had time to move forward into our place. Whatever happened we must not be wiped out before the limited hour had elapsed. After that we could do what we liked. While we waited for Hitler we continued our training on the cliff tops. Room for drilling was very restricted. Our small parade ground was on the Western Heights. There was no barrier between it and the cliff's edge with its savage drop of several hundred feet to the harbour. Whenever it was my turn to be officer on duty there happened to be a sea mist hanging low over the parade ground. Since we drilled each morning, as we did everything else, punctually by the clock the German Messerschmidt fighter pilots soon learnt the precise hour. They much enjoyed diving through the mist, when there was one, over the parade ground and spraying us with machine-gun bullets. Being guardsmen we naturally behaved as though nothing unusual was occurring. But I found that the mist and bullet spray much impaired my vision. Moreover the din made my uncertain words of command less audible than usual.

Having by dint of that repeated effort, which I have already described, got the company on the move I was always haunted by the precipice overlooking the Channel. I greatly admired the adroitness with which the other officers in my company manoeuvred the men backwards and forwards, sideways and diagonally, up to the very lip of the precipice, and then with a flick of the tongue, as it were, whipped them inland in the nick of time. The way in which these nimble witted officers acted and the agile guardsmen reacted was very wonderful to behold. But try as I might I never could achieve it. It was as much as I could do to keep the company sloping arms, or marking time, on the inland side of the square. That could not be maintained indefinitely. And sooner or later I had the chagrin of seeing the men veer Channelwards, and briskly step towards the cliff edge like quicksilver drawn by a magnet. I suppose by some inexplicable contingency they were doing it to my command. So long as the company were fairly within sight all might be well. But once they were away and lost in mist and bullet spray only luck, not skill, could possibly stop them falling like Gadarene swine over the precipice, and being smashed to smithereens on the quay. Once, twice, three times I cried *Halt!* always when they were on the wrong foot. After each misfire the sergeant-major would curse them if they did halt, and praise them if they didn't. The officer, he had to admit, was testing them rather severely. But they knew their duty. Meanwhile he gave me pitying, disdainful and finally furious glances. Only a miracle could come to my rescue now. If only there were time enough heaven might vouchsafe that one of my commands would coincide with the correct foot movement. But time was running out, the cliff was drawing nearer, and my head was in a whirl.

In trying to extricate myself from this harrowing situation my relations with that odious sergeant-major were not unlike those of the King of Hearts with the White Rabbit at the trial over the tarts. '"That's very important," the King said, turning to the jury. They were just beginning to write this down on their slates, when the White Rabbit interrupted: "*Un*important, your Majesty means of course," he said in a very respectful tone, but frowning and making faces at him as he spoke. "Unimportant, of course, I meant," the King hastily said, and went on to himself in an undertone, "impor-tant – unimportant – unimportant – important –" as if he were trying which word sounded best.' For the last time I threw one more hazard – and failed. Then the mist lifted. The Messerschmidt sped back across the Channel. Craning my neck and screwing up my eyes I watched in horror the company march in perfect formation over the precipice to a man. The sergeant-major and I were left alone on the square. He so far forgot himself as to shrug one shoulder in disgust. Silence reigned. At that moment the Colonel and Adjutant walked on to an empty parade ground.

If I had had a loaded revolver in my holster I would without any question have drawn it out and shot myself. 'Where is the company?' the Adjutant asked. 'I thought the men were drilling,' the Colonel said. 'They are, sir,' the sergeant-major answered. 'They were, sir,' I said with my greater regard for accuracy and truth. 'What the hell do you mean?' the Adjutant said. 'I mean that I marched the whole lot over the cliff, sir,' I said. 'I'm most frightfully sorry. I didn't mean to. It was entirely a mistake.'

'The devil it was,' the Colonel said, and to the sergeant-major, 'Get them back again at once. This officer must come and see me at 6 o'clock.' I received the most tremendous rocket for being so conspicuously, so abysmally inefficient. But I avoided disclosing that I was as blind as a bat. Mercifully I was never allowed to drill again at Dover. The guardsmen who were retrieved clinging to tufts of sea thistle and ledges of rock received the highest commendation for their observance of the rules and adherence to discipline in trying circumstances. They had enjoyed themselves no end.

Life at Dover was full of exciting incidents; and fortunately the long intervening stretches of monotony have faded away in retrospect. In the crystalline autumn mornings we would watch from the cliff as though from an opera box our convoys being strafed by German bombers. The ships would hug the coast, but I never saw one of them falter. The implacable determination, the imperturbable slow wake from their huddled forms on the still water, especially at nightfall when the darkness accentuated their lonely peril, nearly moved me to tears.

Daily too we watched the processions of droning Heinkels and Messerschmidts pass over the town at incredible heights and in orderly formation. The A.A. guns barked and sprinkled the blue sky with tufts of cotton wool. The ground we stood on thudded with shell splinters. Hours later we saw the drifting Armadas return, disordered, disarrayed, our Spitfires hot in pursuit. There were plenty of dog fights up above, and it was thrilling to follow with our glasses the white serpents of vapour, four, five miles high, and at their head the tiny gold bees turning, twisting, lunging, and again scrambling upwards, while the whistling strain of engines, and the popping of machine guns like children's crackers reached our ears long afterwards.

Then came the culminating moment, the high hysterical laughter of a bomber disintegrating at twenty-seven thousand feet. Presently the engine would dive elliptically, trailing an oily smoke, meet an angle of the air in its speed, turn and flutter down like a leaf, oh! so slowly and unrealistically. Was it a Hun? Yes, it was. A corporal standing beside me swore that he could recognize, without glasses but with the naked eye, the swastika on a Heinkel's tail as clearly from four miles as the birthmark on his wife's from as many inches. He could never be mistaken. Now engine and propeller had left the wings behind. These wings were zigzagging downwards like sycamore pods through the turquoise dome and into the chalky drum of the horizon. Look! there was the faint grey dot of a parachute hanging stock still in the sky. It would not reach the world for twenty minutes; and the wind was blowing it out to sea.

When the wind had blown it out to sea we had a splendid view from the cliff of the great envelope at eye level drifting, and finally gathering itself upon impact with the waves. The white of the silk and the splashing foam was all one. In the twinkling of an eye an M.T. boat would dash to the rescue, through the breakwater of the harbour, that harbour where twelve months previously the *Maid of Orleans* would have been starting to chug a leisurely passage to Calais.

At night we would see across the Straits a flash from the long-range gun emplacements at Cap Gris-Nez, or Boulogne. Between sixty and seventy seconds later a shell fell, sometimes on the barracks, usually upon the town. The explosion sent a wild olympian echo across the valley, rattling away over the downs. If the shell fell into the sea, which it sometimes did, the explosion was more terrible as though the element had been split asunder. The damage the shells did was in relation to their noise inconsiderable. But we never knew when they were coming, nor how long the canonades would last. Sometimes they would last for three quarters of an hour, with intervals of five minutes between each salvo. The shells were a nuisance rather than an alarm, and eventually necessitated the battalion leaving barracks (the Sergeants' Mess was hit and a few men lost their lives) and sleeping underground.

I was far more worried by the loss of the old buildings of Dover than the lives. I would gladly have offered mine for the preservation of the Regency terraces along the sea front. These elegant, smiling stucco houses, called Waterloo Mansions, with their unbroken curve of iron balconies, stood at the very gateway to England. They were the first domestic architecture of a great epoch of our history to welcome foreign visitors to these shores. They were something to be proud of; and they were only partly damaged by Hitler's weapons of war. When peace was declared they were totally swept away by the aldermen of Dover in token of thanksgiving.

The Grand Shaft Barracks were surrounded by a deep walled moat crossed by a bridge. In the bowels of the chalky cliff tunnels and passages led from bastions into dungeons. These had been constructed by French prisoners of war in Napoleonic times. During the Battle of Britain the guardsmen slept on the stone floor of the dripping dungeons, in which huge peat fires were kept smouldering through the night. Each officer slept with his platoon. On Sunday mornings Mass was said in a catacomb, vaulted like a primitive church in which the early Christians worshipped, and lit by narrow, splayed embrasures in the thick walls. The guardsmen crowded into the galleries, and slung their rifles and bayonets upon hooks in the bare walls. Oil lamps hung on chains from the vaulting, and the air was filled with incense and peat smoke. It amazed me how many of the guardsmen regularly took communion. The Piranesian grandeur of the catacomb and the artless improvisation of the ceremony were most moving.

In October when the invasion scares were over I had my first forty-eight hours' leave, and went home. Both my parents were preoccupied, and exhausted. Night after night my mother, wearing her brother's old tin helmet from the previous war and his long Jaeger dressing-gown, as though these incongruous objects acted as amulets, and a whistle on a string round her neck, paraded the village street with a soda-water siphon, in readiness to put out any incendiary bomb which might alight upon a thatched cottage. My father, now an extremely efficient major in the Home Guard, was sweeping the skies with a telescope on the track of German parachutists in nuns' habits. They were naturally too busy to pay much attention to me. I returned by train to London on a Sunday evening. On arrival at Paddington station I found an air raid in progress. Not a taxi was on the streets. I was to meet some officers at the Bachelors' Club and motor with them down to Dover. There was no alternative to walking to the club. So I put on my steel helmet and because it was dark and not a soul was about to witness my shame, carried my suitcase. On reaching the west side of Hyde Park Square I heard the familiar whine of a falling bomb, ran up the steps and crouched under the portico of a house. What happened thereafter I have only managed to piece together like the small sections of a jigsaw puzzle that have been scattered over the years. Even now I have no clear recollection whatever of the sequence of events.

I think that on this occasion the house behind the portico where I was sheltering received a direct hit. For when I passed the site months later there was a hole where the house had been. Only the portico was left standing. I can just recall picking myself up beside the iron railings of the square garden across the road. The marks on my ribs suggested that I was flung against them. I can also remember crawling about the pavement in circles vainly looking for my steel helmet and gas mask, neither of which were recovered. Their loss was an unnatural worry to me. But I do not remember anything further. Apparently I was perfectly well able to reach the Bachelors' Club where I had a stiff whisky and soda. Apparently my friends drove me to Dover. Apparently the next morning I delivered a lecture to my platoon on the mechanism of the rifle, and was overheard by the Company commander talking gibberish. Apparently in the afternoon I went on a short route march. That evening while changing into my blues for dinner I passed out, and remained in a coma for twenty-four hours.

The following ten months were spent, off and on, in five different hospitals. The symptoms of my recurring trouble, once I came through the initial coma, baffled the specialists of the first four hospitals. For I would be overtaken with brief or long fits of unconsciousness accompanied by spasms of the left leg. On coming round I felt as though I had just lost a hundred yards' sprint and been given a turn or two on the rack as a punishment. There was little satisfaction in being conscious again. After an hour I would be as normal as though nothing had happened. Sometimes but not always, these fits would be preceded by flashes of warning, known as *aura*. I can only describe them as preternatural. For no ascertainable reason, during conversation, in walking, reading, or concentrating, while enjoying myself, or working, and usually when I was not thinking about myself, my mind would become detached from my body. I seemed to be floating in the air. It was not a disagreeable sensation because all subjectivity left me. I was looking down upon the world beneath me from an aerial distance, just as though I were a disembodied spirit, but a spirit devoid of will or purpose, a very junior myrmidon in the host of – was it? – heaven. Yet the sense of detachment was accompanied by one of foreboding. The whole transmogrification lasted a short time, I daresay a few seconds. As suddenly as it happened, it was over. I was myself down below again, but only for a minute. It was then that I soon learned to seek safety without delay, and take refuge wherever that was possible. I would leave the room, or if I were in the street, dash into a shop, or better still, sit or lie on a bench. But this was not always possible. There were awkward and embarrassing visitations in public places, awkward for others and embarrassing for me when I came round.

Once I was stricken on the top of a bus late at night and came to in the terminal depôt miles beyond Battersea long after the last return bus had left for the West End where I was staying. Another time in a taxi, the driver of which, a shocked Plymouth Brother assuming that I was drunk, drove me to Vine Street and pitched me unceremoniously into the Police Station. I was wearing uniform and had difficulty in proving my sobriety. Another time on an island in Piccadilly where, in crossing the street, I had met and was talking to the wife of a Rural Dean whom I knew but slightly. I knocked her down flat and fell on top of her, head to head and tail to tail, while the traffic swerved to avoid us. We were separated, as I learnt later, by a policewoman and an indignant gentleman who rained blows on the back of my head with his umbrella while shouting, 'Disgusting! And in public too! What a place to choose!' In between these fits I was right as rain.

The first hospital treated me for concussion of the brain, the second for compression of the spinal cord, the third for sciatica and the fourth for psychoneurosis. The first three were nearer the mark – I had in fact broken the base of my spine – whereas the fourth merely made me deeply suspicious of psychiatric treatment. A sympathetic doctor can after a month's intimacy make a patient say anything he wishes him to say. I watched my fellow patients wallowing in a form of self-justification by attributing their odious little weaknesses to irrelevant incidents which had befallen them in infancy – a father's cuff on the behind, a nanny's tickling of their naval, a glimpse through a keyhole of a great aunt licking a photograph of Lord Kitchener – and changing from mild eccentrics to confirmed hypochondriacs. My doctor was one of the most cultivated and sympathetic old men I have ever met. When his charm had beaten down my resistance I began to fall under his spell. Twice a day we had fascinating conversations upon every subject under the sun, while I tried ineffectually to parry the only one which bored me, namely myself. There was so little about me which I did not know already, and far better than he ever could. I was however trying, in order not to be too ungracious, to respond to this charming man's pressure, when he dropped down dead of a heart attack. I was deeply affected and mourned a new friend just when I was growing to value and depend upon him, possibly too much.

In the late summer of 1941 I was sent to the Queen Elizabeth Hospital in Birmingham. Here I underwent every sort of test including one by the only encephalograph then in England. This infallible machine diagnosed my complaint as, without any doubt, Jacksonian epilepsy. I had twice suffered from this strange complaint at my preparatory school, without anyone realizing at the time what it was, but not again until the experience in Hyde Park Square resuscitated it. I was appalled. I thought there was something shameful in the word epilepsy, as in lunacy or syphilis, something to be deeply concealed. I was also alarmed – and embarrassed – because my mother suffered from Jacksonian epilepsy throughout her adult life, which was certainly ruined by it. In her case it grew worse from year to year, and she never threw it off. Whether our both being victims was coincidental or hereditary has never been explained to me.

For several years I was incommoded by a series of drugs administered to check the complaint. First one and then another was prescribed. One was so soporific that it was constantly sending me to sleep when I ought to have been awake; another so stimulant that it would not let me sleep without terrifying nightmares. One made me vomit; another acted like ten cocktails and was followed by a violent hangover. One induced euphoria; another suicidal depression. After an experimental period each drug had to be increased in order to stay effective. The cumulative toxins made me so ill that the drug had to be reduced. In consequence I was visited with more fits, sometimes as many as ten a day, reducing me to a state bordering on prostration. Finally a drug was tried which suited, and still suits me. I am never without this golden key to health and happiness. It accompanies me everywhere. Gradually the fits subsided, until they ceased altogether. Yet for nearly thirty years I have been a regular drug addict.

I would like fellow sufferers from Jacksonian epilepsy to derive some encouragement from my case history, to scorn all silly shame and find comfort in the fact that many estimable persons from Hercules to Edward Lear have been afflicted with it. I would like non-sufferers to realize that epileptics, when they are not 'under the influence' of the demon, are just as sane as they, which may not be saying much. I only ask them to make allowance for the epileptic's understandable tendency to agoraphobia. In the long run the complaint is more ridiculous than serious so long as it can be kept within bounds.

In April 1941 I had been discharged from my third hospital. On arrival at my London club I found a letter from Harold Nicolson, then Parliamentary Secretary at the Ministry of Information. It told me that Robert Byron's ship to Alexandria had been torpedoed and that he was drowned. Robert, from whom a month or two ago I had parted on bad terms. I had gone to say good-bye to him in the Paddington Hotel. I was in uniform. He was in a highly nervous state, and began inveighing against his bugbear, Lord Lloyd, who as Secretary of State for the Colonies had recently died in office, much to my distress. I told him that for a very clever man he could be remarkably silly. Descending in the lift to the ground floor he gave me a smart clout on the cheek which knocked off my cap. An American lady who had entered the lift with us was greatly shocked to see a plethoric civilian assaulting an officer in the Brigade. My dignity was affronted and I was furious. As we got out of the lift I said, 'I shall never see you again, Robert. This is the end' – meaning nothing of the sort. But it was.

With Harold's letter in my pocket and sadness in my heart I went to the Spanish Majorca restaurant to dine with Peter Montgomery. It was my first dinner out for a long time. It coincided with the beginning of the worst raid of the war on London, in which 2,300 people were killed and 3,000 seriously injured. At ten o'clock a bomb dropped in our street, shattering the front of the restaurant. When Peter and I stepped on to the pavement there was a fiendish noise overhead. I knew that I could not get to

Chelsea where I was supposed to stay. I could not walk so far, and no buses or taxis were running. Peter likewise had a long way to go home. We decided to take refuge in the nearest hotel we could find. We crept along walls, plunged across Regent Street and entered the Piccadilly Hotel where we drank until midnight. The raid getting worse we took a room on the fifth floor. There were nine floors in the hotel, and all the rooms on the lower were already taken. We half-undressed and quailed in our beds until 2 a.m. The bombs were hailing, swishing down on all sides so that sleep was out of the question. The explosions and the rattle of retaliatory gunfire were deafening. We dressed again and went downstairs. Peter left his khaki overcoat and I my Sam Browne belt in the bedroom. Downstairs we felt perfectly safe, for the Grill Room was two floors below street level. As we passed through the entrance hall we saw slices of thick plate glass strewn upon the carpets. The revolving doors had blown in.

Less than twenty minutes later the first bomb hit the hotel. The building shivered and a fine dry dust filled the air and made people sneeze. Men and women caught like us were sprawling as men and women sprawl at night time in railway carriages with their mouths wide open, on the floors and stairs. We stood, sat and wandered in the lower basement where, apart from an occasional thump and tremor, nothing indicated how the raid was proceeding. At intervals we climbed to street level to find out. Once I put my head out of doors. A gust of blast met me. I retreated. There was no point in courting death. Not long afterwards while we were below again, a second bomb fell on the hotel with a loud repercussion. It was like a thunder clap above our heads. I was pitched off my chair. While the foundations rocked and swayed there was time to screw my body like a hedgehog into a protective ball against the masonry crumbling, rumbling down the marble staircase. Were we to be crushed, buried alive, underground? A cataract of boulders was arrested by a grand piano. A smashing, slashing of glass and wood followed in its wake. Nothing further. The lights went out. Officious men's voices shouted, 'Keep calm!' Everyone kept calm.

There was a stifling smell of cordite and the acrid stench of plaster and stale wallpaper. When torches were flashed on nothing was visible but blobs of light behind a fog of black, curling smoke. I feared I would choke and for a foolish second thought of poison gas. There was a rending cacophony of spluttering and coughing. Spitting.

Before the smell and dust subsided, a third bomb fell on the Piccadilly pavement just beside the wall against which we were crouching below. I was saying rather querulously, 'Peter, where are you?' because his companionship was at that moment very dear to me. He lit a torch and there he stood as sartorially elegant and serene as ever. Only one lock of hair drooped over an eyebrow; and his forehead was puckered because he does not care to be dishevelled. It is symptomatic of ill-breeding on somebody's part. The Germans. And now they were at it again. Crash! We were thrown by this fresh exhibition of outrageous manners clumsily against each other. This time Peter frowned without attempting to check himself. I said, 'I have mislaid my gas mask', and Peter flashed his torch upon the ground through the whiskings and flickerings of the black dust. Then I laughed aloud. It did seem odd. My gas mask was floating upon a stream, borne beneath a plush sofa. The last bomb had hit a water main outside the hotel. Our ankles were immersed in a yellow slime. People were clambering upon gold, cane-seated chairs above the swirling stream, the women knotting their skirts about their middles. Men appeared with brooms. Someone opened a manhole and the noisy torrent – for it was that now – was directed into it.

So we paddled, frisked and waded knee deep from chair to chair, or hopped upon one, using another like a stilt, for as the torrent altered its course, there was the likelihood of being marooned on one chair and unable to communicate with a shallower bottom save by swimming. And it was still early spring, in England.

At five o'clock the all-clear sounded. Peter – his tie was out of place – and I clambered through rubble, up broken flights of stairs, down semi-blocked corridors, over fallen girders, and through dislocated doorways to our bedroom. The second bomb had exploded in the suite next to ours. Our two beds were still recognizable, although mine was facing the wrong way, turned back to front and the iron chassis of the thing twisted like a whiting. The rest of the furniture and fittings, the cupboards, tables and window frames were not so recognizable. A cloth of lumpish grey was a shroud to the room. From under a hummock Peter disinterred his overcoat. He held it at arm's length and blew upon it. I did not recover my Sam Browne belt.

Piccadilly resembled a giant skeleton asleep upon an ice floe. The eye sockets of the houses looked reproachfully at the dawn. Like lids, torn blinds and curtains fluttered from every window. The brows of windows and portals were wrenched and plucked. On pavement and street a film of broken glass crunched under the feet like the jagged crystals of slush icicles. One had to take care that they did not clamber over the edge of one's shoes. The contents of shop windows were strewn over the pavements among the broken glass. Silk shirts and brocaded dressing-gowns fluttered upon area railings. The show case of a jeweller's window had sprinkled tray-loads of gold watches and bracelets as far as the curb of the street. I stooped to pick up a handful of diamonds and emeralds – and chuck them back into the shop before they got trodden on, or looted.

The sky had the gunmetal solidity of sky before a snow storm. Cinders showered upon our hair, faces and clothes. On all sides columns of smoke sprang from raging fires, the glint of whose flames could be seen above the rooftops, trembling upon chimney stacks and burnishing the dull surface of the sky. I was reminded of Pepys's description of the Great Fire of London in 1666, 'a most horrid malicious bloody flame, not like the fine flame of an ordinary fire.'

A cinder fell into the corner of Peter's eye and caused him pain. The eye smarted and watered. He was very good and followed me around. I wished to see all the damage there might be, to be saddened and maddened thereby. We could not walk up Piccadilly, because a stick of bombs having fallen from the Fifty Shilling Tailors to St James's Church had penetrated a gas main. Tongues of flame were belching from craters in the road. We could not walk down Jermyn Street which was blocked by rubble from collapsed houses. Here I noticed the stripped, torn trunk of a man on the pavement. Further on I picked up what looked like the mottled, spread leaf of a plane tree. It was a detached hand with a signet ring on the little finger.

We passed down Lower Regent Street, through Charles Street and into St James's Square. An alarming fire was raging behind the London Library. I feared for the Library, but this time it escaped harm. That was to come three years later when I was again in London and helped form a human chain of salvagers. I stood on a girder projecting over a well and threw books from the theological department to a neighbour.

Peter and I now passed down King Street. The fire in Christie's was wonderful and awful. The façade still stood and the empty windows revealed a turgid, golden tissue of flame. The fire roared like a giant voraciously eating. Nothing in the world could have stopped it. Strips of lacquer cabinet, the back of a Chippendale settee, wads of horsehair stuffing, the leg of a refectory table hurtled into the air and fell around our feet.

The pale windows of Arthur's Club in St James's Street were aglow with the reflection of yet another fire. For a moment I thought this fine classical building was blazing. Then I realized that the light was not Pepys's 'horrid malicious bloody' sort, but borrowed and deceptive, the sort of light that greets one from the flickering log fire of a hall seen through the crinkled panes of a country house, as one returns before curtains are drawn after a long autumn walk, having crossed the park, about to tread the mossy lawn, late for tea in the Midlands. We were drawn towards the end of Little St James's Street. The attics of Bridgewater House were burning. The flames were smashing the windows with a horsewhip crack from inside, licking the outside walls and trying to fold their thongs round the chimneystacks. I fumbled with the handle of the front door, for I wanted to warn the caretaker. It was locked and bolted. A policeman put a hand on my shoulder and warned me off. 'All the contents were removed long ago, chum,' he said, with a knowing wink. I turned my back on the fate of Barry's masterpiece which was not, as it turned out, disastrous. My face and hair were scorched by another furnace across the road, a magnificent and sad spectacle. A sooty brick Georgian house in a silent corner of its own was turned into a devilish cauldron. A deep bow front with Trafalgar balconies acted like an enormous grate. The draught through the empty windows blew the fire into a ball of seething worms. The roof had gone and one long, thick, blackened beam raised a charred arm rhythmically up and down across the skyline, as though imprecating a dying curse upon our civilization; after a while it withdrew, leaving one calcined finger pointing threateningly. The finger too disappeared into the cauldron.

I was made wretched by the destruction of so many beautiful buildings in a quarter of London which I knew intimately. I thought of my contrasting indifference to good architecture during the first air raid I experienced. This was in 1918 when I was at school. One night I was not sleeping and the dormitory was as quiet as a mausoleum. Something made me creep out of bed, feel for my slippers and dressing gown, and speed across the floor to the window. I lifted up the blind gently, and peered into the night. It was a little misty out of doors, but the moon was up. Scattered clouds were floating in the sky like dinghies on a lake. I listened, and heard through the crisp glass a faint droning. Enough! I knew what it must be, let the blind fall, retreated and found my way surreptitiously out of the dormitory, up the forbidden stairway to the platform where cisterns hissed and moths battered their antennae against naked rafters. There was a trapdoor that unlatched silently. I stepped on to the flat roof between two gables where the flagpole soared above the balustrade, the school flagpole which was normally flagless, but on Parents' Day flew a union jack seemingly no bigger than a handkerchief, but covering quite a third of the cricket pitch when Mrs Burgess, the headmaster's wife, patched it in the summer holidays.

I perched on the balustrade between the two gables, letting my feet rest securely on the tiles. Down below I could see to my right the long passageway roofed with corrugated iron which led to the separate house where the headmaster, Mrs Burgess and their horrid children lived. It was a perfect little Queen Anne house of red brick with a white wooden porch, cupola and pretty weather vane. It had however no charms for me. Up above, one searchlight swept the sky nervously, and another was quietly prizing open a cloud like a coffin lid. In listening carefully I distinguished a deep, worried, hunted drone from several shrill, chirruping, teazing drones. I jumped off the balustrade and knelt on the cold leads. Putting my hands together I prayed fervently. 'Dear God, shoot down that zeppelin on to the headmaster's house. But spare the school annexe, for Jesus Christ's sake. Amen.'

This is what I recollect of a night's intense excitement. Next morning all the boys were taken to see a crinkled, webbed skeleton of twisted steel, undulating upon the downs. They were, I remember, much gratified. I was secretly rather disappointed.

In September 1941 I was discharged from my fifth hospital. After an interval I returned to work with the National Trust. My military career had been inglorious. My illness was humiliating. I was disappointed with myself, and also deeply depressed by the turn the war had taken. The midsummer day on which while lying in bed in hospital I listened to Churchill on the radio magnifying the virtues of our new ally, Soviet Russia, marks without any question the nadir of my whole life. No situation, I then thought, could be more perilous to a nation's soul than that in which to save its skin it has no alternative to compromising with the devil. Was salvation at this price worth the candle? Ever since the 22nd of June, 1941 I have been convinced that evil is not just the negation of good, but the more potent of the two polarities between which our fortunes revolve, and that existence on earth is of small intrinsic value. Since this life is clearly a losing battle of good against evil I hope, without being at all sure, that the next may offer some opportunity of identification with the eternal truths, of which the Almighty has so far merely vouchsafed us a transient glimpse.

I was sustained at this time – and indeed for just over a year longer – by perhaps the most intimate and delicious friendship of the many with which I have been blessed. I never saw her. I never knew who she was. I was to call her Egeria because like that nymph she was so elusive, and she so quickly melted into tears and laughter. It was not of course her real christian name. Inevitably she called me Numa, the mortal who accepted Egeria's instructions in the art of living.

Late one night in London, during an in-between hospital period, I was endeavouring to telephone to a friend. Instead of getting through to him my line was crossed with that of a woman, also wanting to telephone. 'My number is Grosvenor 8527,' I heard her tell the operator, 'and I want a Hampstead number. Instead of which you have hitched me up to Flaxman something. This poor man doesn't want to talk to me at all.' 'Oh yes, I do,' I joined in, for I liked her voice immensely. It was harmonious and clever. Instead of being cross this woman was very good humoured about the muddle. After mutual apologies we both rang off. A minute or two later I dialled again, and again got on to her, although there was no resemblance between her number and the one I was trying to get. Since it seemed that our lines were predestined to link up, we talked to each other for twenty minutes. 'Why were you wanting to speak to a friend after midnight, anyway?' she asked. I told her the reason which I have now forgotten. 'And why were you?' I asked her. She explained that her old mother slept badly, and she often talked to her late at night. Then we discussed the books we were reading, and of course the war. Finally I said, 'I don't remember enjoying a talk so much for years.' 'It was fun, wasn't it? Well I suppose we ought to stop now,' she said. 'I suppose we must. Good-bye.' 'Good night,' she said. 'Pleasant dreams.'

All next day I thought of our conversation. I thought of her intelligent remarks about Balzac. I thought of her spontaneity, her enthusiasm, and her sense of fun. I thought too of her distinctive

accent which was soft and seductive, without being the least insinu-
ating. Its musical modulation haunted me. I am not good at
remembering telephone numbers, but for some reason Grosvenor
8527 stuck. I kept repeating it to myself in buses and on pavements,
and I wrote it down for fear of forgetting.

That evening in bed I paid little attention to what I was reading.
By midnight Grosvenor 8527 was recurring so often in my head
that I could bear it no longer. I got up, went to the telephone and
with trepidation dialled the number. I heard the swift, disengaged
purr of the bell at the other end, the note that was soon to become
as familiar and welcoming as the high-pitched, frenzied engaged
signal was rebarbative. In course of time I got to know by the pitch
of the very first ring whether she was at home, or not. If she was at
home the ring was warm and joyous. If she was away, it took on a
hollow sound like a desolate voice crying for mercy in a tomb. The
longer one let it continue the more deathlike and tragic it sounded.
On this occasion however the receiver at the other end was picked
up instantly, as it always was to be when she was there. 'Hello! it's
me. So sorry to be a bore, but may we continue our conversation
where we left off last night?' I asked. Without saying no or yes, she
straightway launched upon a dissertation on *La Cousine Bette*
which was highly original and funny. Within minutes we were
joking and laughing as though we had known each other for years.

This time we talked for three quarters of an hour. She was
enchanting. The late hour and our anonymity broke down all those
absurdly conventional reserves which usually hedge two people
during preliminary meetings after an introduction. At the end of
this talk I suggested that we ought to introduce ourselves. But she
would not have it. It might spoil everything, she said. 'I don't recognize your voice, nor you mine. If we found that we had friends or
even relations in common, there would be a restraint upon our
totally unguarded talks. Let's not even mention our friends by
name in case one of us has a clue who the other may be.' Her only
concession was to make a note of my telephone number.

We had several more midnight talks before I went to the

Birmingham hospital from which I occasionally rang her up in London. But from a public call-box trunk calls, which must necessarily be short, were not as satisfactory as local ones which could last as long as we wanted them to. Before I left for Birmingham I extracted a promise from her that we would reveal our identities when the war ended. Even so she gave it with some reluctance. All I ever learned about her circumstances was that she had been married at seventeen to a disagreeable man from whom she was separated. She was thirty-six. Her only child had recently been killed flying at the age of eighteen. He meant everything to her and she spoke of him as though he were still alive. After a month or two I got to know him almost as well as her, and found myself saying things like, 'Do you remember how Billy flew over Hamburg and couldn't bring himself to release his bombs over the suburbs?'; or, 'It seems to me that remark of yours was just how Billy would have expressed it.' His was an infinitely endearing personality; and he became like a son to me. Since she once described him as being beautiful as the dawn, and another time as resembling her in every feature, I had a picture of her which once formed never changed. When I told her how beautiful she was to contemplate, she merely laughed and asked, 'How do you know I am?'

We grew to depend upon each other. There were no subjects we did not discuss. Our views on most were identical, including the war. She gave me counsel and strength. The only fault I could find in her was an over-scrupulosity in her relations with others, in particular her husband towards whom her loyalty and help seemed excessive. We took to reading the same books for the fun of discussing them, and because we both belonged to the London Library each undertook not to find out from the librarians the name of the other. When I was discharged from hospital for good I rented a minute house in Chelsea for the rest of the war. Never a night passed when we were both in London that we did not telephone, no matter how late she or I might be back from dinner, and sometimes I was horribly late. I would look forward to our next talk the whole preceding day. If I went away for the weekend and was unable to telephone she complained that she could hardly get to sleep for loneliness. At times I found it unbearable not to see her. I would threaten to jump into a taxi and drive to her at once. 'Let's stop this pantomime. We know each other now better than any couple in the world. And we love each other as much.' But she would not give in. She said that if we met and found we did not love, as then we did, it would kill her. 'Perhaps,' she said, 'I made a mistake in the first place. Now it's too late.' 'All right, my darling,' I said, 'I won't come. Anyway I can't, so long as you refuse to tell me who or where you are. But the war shows little sign of ending. And we may have ages to wait.'

Whenever there was a bad raid at night I would ring up, after it was over, to find out how she was. This always amused her. But I noticed that whenever she imagined there was one over Chelsea she did the same. When my telephone was out of order I would send a telegram addressed simply to Grosvenor 8527 and signed Numa, just to say that I was alive. And whenever my work took me out of London for a few days I felt anxious.

For twelve months I lived in an extraordinary state of inner content. Extraordinary because the times through which we were living were grim, and our love was in a sense unfulfilled. But it had compensations. It was the first I ever experienced that lacked agony. There was nothing to provoke a twinge of jealousy, that terrible and almost invariable accompaniment of love which undermines the spirit. I knew that our osmosis was entirely free from the usual shoals and reefs that beset the turbulence of passion. There seemed no reason why it should not flow on this even course for ever. After all, the language of words is more fervent and more enduring than that of the eyes, or the hands.

But the sable of fate's brooding wings is intensified by the contrasting brightness of the heavens in which the innocent prey are disporting themselves. Fate struck swiftly. One night I got back to London late from the country. I picked up the receiver and dialled her number. Instead of the clear, healthy ringing tone, instead of the high-pitched and hysterical engaged signal, there was a prolonged, piercing scream. I can never listen to that signal now without feeling faint. It means the line is out of order, or the line no longer exists at all. Next day the same banshee scream was repeated. And the next. No telegram signed Egeria came. In great distress I asked Enquiries to find out what had happened. I begged them to give me the address of Grosvenor 8527 even at the risk of breaking my solemn promise to her. The number was, I knew, ex-directory in order to prevent the husband's unwelcome attentions. At first Enquiries would say nothing. They thought it odd that I could not even tell them the subscriber's name. Finally an obliging operator agreed for once to disregard Post Office regulations. After all, she said, why should she not oblige me? 'We may all be blown sky high any moment. And you seem worried. The fact is that the house to which this number belonged received a direct hit three nights ago. There can be no harm now in giving you the sub-scriber's name.'

'Thank you,' I said, 'for your help. I would much rather you didn't. So please, please don't.' And I rang off.